2019

2019

A YEAR IN VERSE

Douglas Palermo

2019
A YEAR IN VERSE

iUniverse books may be ordered through booksellers or by contacting:

iUniverse
1663 Liberty Drive
Bloomington, IN 47403
www.iuniverse.com
1-800-Authors (1-800-288-4677)

ISBN: 978-1-5320-9468-2 (sc)
ISBN: 978-1-5320-9467-5 (e)

Library of Congress Control Number: 2020902386

Print information available on the last page.

iUniverse rev. date: 02/06/2020

January 1st

Are you waiting
For the bathroom
Bud?

No.

I'm waiting
For my bud
In the bathroom.

Teal
Swanning.

Stride forward.

What else
Can I
Say?

All
Apologies.

You
Are
Forgiven.

January 2nd

Back to work.

Building the
Future.

The ethers
Are
Getting
Thick.

But I am
Rising
Above them.

Shouldering
The burden.

This
Is not
My first
Rodeo.

This
Is when
I'm at
My best.

January 3rd

God
In disguise.

Doing it
For kicks.

Alan
Watts up?

Dave
Visit.

The rest
Is a mirage
Because
It contained
Too much
Reality.

That doctor
Was cute.

I think
She was
Checking
Me out.

I am
Beginning
To be
Recognized.

January 4th

Forgotten night.

Routines
Not
Solidified.

Morning after
Recovery.

No one
Is
The wiser.

A decade
Of
Jake.

A cascade
Of
Cakes.

Laughing
And
Joy.

Family
Are those
In
Your life.

January 5th

Upstairs?

Downstairs?

Hanging
By a
Thread.

Will
It
Survive?

Agitation.

Frustration.

Still laying
The groundwork.

The cement
Will
Be dried
Soon.

Then
It is time
To
Keep
Building.

January 6th

Returning
Home.

Reaching
An epiphany.

New moons
And
Eclipses.

The dissertation
Is
Completed.

The stage
Is
Cleared.

A New
Vibration
Has
Been
Earned.

Enjoy it.

Use it
Well.

For the saints
Are
Marching
In.

Seeds planted
Coming to
Full
Bloom.

Grateful.

Blessed.

I love
My new
Life.

I love
My new
Light.

Now
I need
To
Make up
For
Lost time.

Enjoy
The fruits
Of labor.

Enjoy
Labor.

Enjoy.

Such is
Life.

Flat tire.

Growing
Desire.

It took
Us
Long
Enough.

Time
To bring it
In
For
A landing.

Rumors.

Handle
With grace.

Let's give
Them
Something
To talk
About.

I would
Love
To forget
About it
As I
Help
You
Remember it
All.

January 9th

Standardized
Tested.

Particles
Not waves.

You
Can't
Do it
Alone.

Definitely
Sting
It.

Ethers grow
Thick.

The vibration
Strengthens
But
Slows.

Slip
Into the
Background
Again.

January 10th

Beauty
In the
Mist
Of the
Dense
Reality.

Lightness.

Six
At work.

Seven
In the
E.R.

Now
I am
On a
Different
Planet.

Bathing
In
Sound.

Resiliency.

We got it
In spades.

Grit.

More
Than a
Duck's
Worth.

The adventure
Soundtrack
Or
The soundtrack
To the
Adventure?

A
Sonic
Parade.

Hide
Your thoughts
While
Speaking
Your mind.

Your actions
Tell
Your story.

Show
And
Prove.

The time
Travelling
Gondola
Awaits.

Waging
Hope.

Circling
The wagons.

Finding
Stability.

A day
Of
Firsts.

A lifetime
Of
Lasts.

The familiar
Shore
Is
Fading in
The horizon.

These are
New
Waters.

Navigate them
With all
You
Have learned.

The Holy
Man
Is
Dying.

As
We all
Recount
The lessons
Learned.

A trip
Comes to
An end
Through
The release
Of
Climax.

You
Should
Be dancing.

You have
Known that
Already.

Go out
And
Find
A Stage
To
Dance on.

January 14th

Back
To work.

Embracing
The new
Normal.

Life
Is
Hard.

But
It is
Easier
When
You
Feel good.

The edge
Of
The blade
Is
Dulling.

But still
I stand
Like
A rock.

Spreading
Butter
Instead of
Slicing
Meat.

January 15th

On
The brink.

Trying to
Get him
Back home.

A forgotten
Birthday.

Old friends
Fade.

New ones
Emerge.

Preparing
For
What is
Ahead.

Not looking
At the
Left
Behind.

You
Only get
So many chances
To prove
Who
You are
As
A human
Being.

January 16th

Mouth swabbing.

Are
We out
Of the
Woods
Yet?

Change is
Constant.

Changes are
Fast.

Letting go
Is easy
When
You just
Drop
It.

The storms
Are
Brewing.

What
Will they
Bring?

Hail
To
The Chiefs!

He's dead.

Wanting
To be
Alone.

A journey
Ends.

A Torch
Is
Dampened
While a
New flame
Is lit.

Toughness
Revealed.

The saints
Come marching
In.

So proud
To be
Part of
That number.

An energetic
Transfer.

What
Day of
The week
Is it?

All
A blur?

Woo.

Who?

Diabetic priest
With the Mac
And
Cheese.

Fruity Pebbles
On
A donut.

Mike Tyson
And
Tigers.

All
A blur.

The salt
Of
The earth.

Generator
Of
House sounds.

Never
Say goodbye.

January 19th

Seeking normalcy.

Embracing
The everyday
Things.

The storm
Comes.

But
It is
Dealt with.

Stories emerge.

The legend
Grows.

A boomerang
Of
Love
And
Kindness.

Returning
To
The spot

It was
Launched.

This is
Moving
Forward.

January 20th

A full moon.

A lunar
Eclipse.

The games
Are
Extended.

More time
To be
Disappointed.

Dipping into
An over-used
Well.

These are
New
Times.

Dig in
New
Ground.

Find a
New
Spring.

The old
Ways
Are
Done.

Passing
The baton.

A changing
Of
The guard.

Not
The best
Scenario
But for
The best.

The process
Of
Processing
Begins.

After
The storm
But
Far from
Calm.

One more
Big hurdle
To cross.

I know
I can
Do it.

January 22nd

An early
Morning
Escape.

Off to
Play
While
The pain
And sadness
Returns.

Chaos comes
From
The south.

The Queen
Retreats
To
Her castle.

The knights
Ready
Their defense.

Prepare!

A proper
Send off.

Practice
Makes
Perfect.

Hitting
The triple
Crown.

Don't stop
Believing.

A simple
Man.

In
A small
Town.

Finding
A New
Home
For Gandhi.

You can
Always
Teach
An old cat
Some
New tricks.

January 24th

A day
After
Funk.

A dark
Driving
Rain.

Struggling to
Get out
Of
The fog.

Gassing up
In more ways
Than
One.

Nobody
Said it
Would
Be easy.

What
I am
Letting go
Of
Is
Hanging on
Tightly.

Need
To Clip
Its
Claws.

January 25th

Getting better
As the day
Progresses.

Letting go
Of
Grudges.

Honoring
Blank slates.

He shoots
He scores.

Again
And
Again.

Showing what
I
Can do.

But
The win
Goes to
The birthday
Girl.

Don't
Let them
Tell you
That you
Can't go
Home again.

January 26ᵗʰ

Crashing
Back down
To Earth.

Body
Fails me.

I just
Want
To be
Cut
A break.

Whose
New normal
Is this?

Continuing
To
Chop wood.

Continuing
To
Carry Water.

Is this all
Just
Some Sisyphean
Task?

Or
Will I
Get
The rock
Over
The hill?

A letter
From Paul.

Jokes
From
The altar.

It is
Not
About
The parts.

It is
About
The whole
Body.

The depression
Sinks
In.

Trying
To crawl
My way
Out.

Asking for
Help.

Being
Forsaken.

Why?

January 28th

A license
Renewed.

How
Poetic.

More
Storms brewing.

They are
For
Other people's
Karmas.

I am
Done
Being
Tested.

The trial
Is
Adjourned.

It was a
No
Contest.

Innocent
Of being
Guilty.

Guilty
Of being
Innocent.

Happy birthday
Brother.

January 29th

Cavities
Filled.

Fish
Gutted.

No gloves
But plenty
Of love.

No need
To numb
The pain.

I came
Here
To feel
It all.

And
I have.

As always
I arrive
To the party
Early.

Everyone else
Is stuck
In traffic.

Awkward
Conversations with
The hosts.

Who
Invited
That guy?

January 30th

The eve
Before
The final
Leap.

The natives
Are
Getting restless.

The crew
Lifts
The anchor.

Here
Comes
The tug.

Feel
The cold
Wind.

There can
Only be
So many
Delays.

The ambassador
Gets caught
Up in
The emotion
Of
The spectacle.

An overseas
Account.

January 31st

A month
In
The books.

Tragedy
And
Triumph.

Can't be
Bottled up
Any longer.

You are
Going
To hear
Me
Roar.

Whether
You like
It
Or not.

Better
Get used to
It.

Hopefully
It will
Be laughter.

Finally winning
A hard fought
After
Joy.

So
Do not
Get in
The way
Of it.

A bear
On
The loose.

A good omen.

A long
Day
Ending
A longer
Week
To
Start off
The shortest
Month.

Pulling
All the threads
Together.

Trying
To make
A rope.

To
Bind with
Not to
Hang.

It is not
My turn
To make
Deals
Yet.

Spidey sense
Is
Tingling.

This
Calls for
A killer
Back hand.

Get
Those juices
Flowing.

Dancing
Between
Angels
And
Animals.

Transcending
And
Including both.

A late night
Cure
For a
Freezeout.

Thaw
Baby
Thaw.

All's well
That ends
Well?

Picking up
The pieces.

You must
Bless
The neck.

Protect it
From
The blaze.

A long line
Of
Sorrow.

An interloper
Of
Grief.

Small gestures
Have
Big meanings.

They
Will not
Grow old.

Longtime friends.

Veterans
Of
Many Wars.

Adjusting
To
Civilian life.

I must have
Release.

February 4th

The cat
Powers.

Through
The tiny
Desk.

Fresh out
Among
The hung
Over.

Apples
Don't fall
Far from
The tree.

But apples
Are sweet.
And trees
Can be
Rough.

Working
It all
Out.

This is
Not
What
Everybody
Signed up
For.

But I
Most certainly
Did.

February 5th

Pronoia is
The antidote
To
Paranoia.

I need to
Put that in
My
Piggy bank.

Taking care
Of
Business.

Turning over
A new
Moon.

A glimpse
Of spring
Yet
Many remain
Spiritually
Frozen.

Do
Your work

And go
Home.

That place
Is just
A dojo.

February 6th

A circle
Of
Trust.

Chilling
With
My peeps.

Being
Easy.

Commuting
Between
Two worlds.

Trying
To maintain
The same
Wavelength
On
Different frequencies.

Some static
Should
Be expected.

Just ignore
All the noise
And
Keep shooting.

February 7th

In the middle
Of
The Tao.

There is
A butterfly.

Tangled up
In
Blue.

Bringing joy
To
The world
Because
We certainly are
The champions.

Familiar faces
Greet me
As I exit
Through
The tunnel.

Where
Have you been
Hiding?

Goodnight
John.

February 8ᵗʰ

A week.
Exhausted.

An exhausting
Week.

Cracking
A lot of
Eggs
While trying
To build
The future.

Sometimes
You have to
Let the mold
Run
Its course.

We will all
Feel
Better
In the morning.

As the wind
Howls

And the temperatures
Drop.

It is
Still
Winter.

A lot of running
Around.

Figuratively
And
Literally.

Carb loaded.

Feeling
Bloated.

Boys
Are now
Men.

Touches of grey
Rule
The day.

Before
A night of
Memories.

Picture postcards
From
A long
Strange trip.

Finding
The balance
Between
Socially awkward
And
Awkwardly social.

February 10th

Hello again.

Finding
Comfort in
The anchor
Of tradition.

Raising
The level
Of dialogue.

Continuing
The process
Of processing.

Taking control
Of
The narrative.

Running
The path
Of
Triumphant redemption.

Timeless monuments
Of the past
Remain.

But now
Is all
That's real.

February 11ᵗʰ

To do
Or not
To do?

That is
The question.

Make a list.

Check it
Twice.

Can you
Stomach
The haze?

Feeling like
A stranger.

In a home
You helped
Build.

Just
Abide.

The pendulum
Will swing
Back.

It is
A state of
Emergency.

So
You can
Turn off
Your alarms.

There is
No bottom
To this.

So
It is time
To move
On.

A chance
Encounter.

God is
No longer
Giving
Any
Wiggle room.

Luckily
I have
Grown weary
Of wiggling.

A portrait
Of
The artist.

Digging through
The past.

Shoveling
A path.

My surrender
And rebirth
Will
Be confirmed.

February 13th

Not feeling
It
Or just
Feeling
Too much
Of it.

An overused turn
Of the phrase.

I have been
Awake
For
Too long.

The flowers
Are not
As fresh
And
The garbage
Just keeps
Piling up.

Thanks
For reaching
Out

But
Forgive me
For wanting to
Hide in
My shell.

Protect me
From
The friendly
Fire.

February 14ᵗʰ

A helpless victim.

Subject
To the whims
Of the day.

Only after
His
Daily bread.

Not realizing
His
Greater purpose.

Yet
Fully prepared.

Filling cracks
In
The foundation.

Ready
To build
A home.

A pirate
Comes ashore.

An anticipatory game
Set
And match.

February 15th

A successful transport.

Curiosity compels
The cat.

A new chapter
In a
New home.

Stars
Of character
Shine brightly.

Achieving goals
While
Enjoying
The play.

My ghost
Continues to
Travel far
As
My mind
And body
Struggle
To keep
Up.

February 16th

Setting
The rules.

Maintaining
Discipline.

But enjoying
The freedom.

Getting lost
In
Another's fantasy
World.

Maintaining
It.

Listening
To others'
Stories.

Willingly playing
Their games.

An early morning
Run.

Cold air
Opening
The lungs.
The sun
Rises
On
Us.

February 17ᵗʰ

Hung
Over heaven.

For all
Of
Hell
To see.

The best
Gamble
Is to
Wager
Nothing
And
Just enjoy
The show.

A month in
The books.

Legacy
Cemented.

Hits
After
Hits.

The knee
Buckles
Under all
The weight.

The storm leaves
With barely
A trace.

February 18th

A lazy day
Sitting on
My high
Horse.

Unable
To go back
In for
A safe landing.

The river
Is our
Only option.

The ferryman
Awaits
Our arrival.

There was
No human
Error.

But
Many doubters
Trying to
Muffle
The sound.

The light
Of
The moon
Will
Expose them.

February 19ᵗʰ

Project based
Grieving.

The wounds
Are
Running deep
But
We are
Getting to
The source.

Scrubbing
The toilet
Clean.

It's
Child's play.

The scaffolding
Of
The celebration.

A clear
Vision
Supported by
Divine love
Cannot lose.

It is why
We are
The champions.

February 20th

A late night
Session.

As
The clean-up
Continues.

The old
Well
Is
Drying up.

But the new
Well
Is
Overflowing.

The line forms
Of those
Ready to
Draw
From it.

Thirst
Is
Rampant.

Come
Get your
Gatorade
For
The soul.

Then take
Your seat
And
Enjoy
God's Art
Show.

Peaceful
Easy feelings.

Helps
To deal
With
Others' turmoil.

He may not
Be heavy
But
I still don't want to
Carry him.

Or
Have him
Pull
Me down.

Faith and fighting
Got me
Up
The mountain.

Where
The promised land
Is visible.

And
Nobody will
Cloud
My vision.

As I walk
Confidently
Forward.

February 22ⁿᵈ

A carefully
Wrapped body.

Survives
The speed
Of
The trip.

All
The pieces
Are now in
Place.

A new Earth
Prepared to
Flourish.

The long
Running game
Is ended.

There are
No real
Winners.

But some
Sore
Losers.

There is
No going
Back.

Stop trying
To grasp
The exhaust
Of
Now.

February 23rd

Chance encounters.

To lift
The spirits.

Orchestrated
From beyond.

I am
Fitting in
Less
And less.

But I feel
Fine.

Living
My truth.

Unapologetic.

Doesn't always
Feel
Great
But
I feel
Better.

Responding
To
Challenges.

Conquering
All
These hills.

Pleasures
Of the flesh.

A path
With
No bottom.

Just
Eternal
Sinking.

The only way
To win
The battle
Is to not
March
Anymore.

The slate
Has been
Washed clean.

The winds
Of change
Are
Fiercely blowing.

Wake up.

Grow up.

And
Show up.

That's half
The battle.

Paul Godmore.

On the road
To Damascus.

After persecuting
The Christ-followers
Within.

Freedom
Without discipline
Is
Slavery.

Time to
Unshackle
Yourself.

The consequences
Of
Excessive
Free will
Are
Predetermined.

Time to
Stick to
Your chosen
Path.

Follow
Jesus.

No looking
Back.

February 26ᵗʰ

Back on
Track.

After
Trips around
The world.

Returning to
The Word.

No need
To keep
Knocking myself down
Just to
Get back
Up.

That muscle
Is
Overworked.

Stay up.

Be
Radically honest.

Some books
Can be
Judged by
Their covers.

Others
By
Their reach.

I just
Keep turning
The page.

February 27th

Controlling anger
Over what
I
Can't control.

We all
Fall short
Of
His glory.

But He
Still smiles
At us.

Granting us
Small victories
And
Continued nourishment.

His will
Is all
We'll do.

Whether we
Like it
Or not.

The ultimate price
Of
Admission.

Some weights
Are
Too heavy
To carry.

Sometimes
Bitterness
Is
Too deep
Rooted
To be
Sweetened.

Feelings
Are
Never wrong
Even when
They are
Unwelcome.

I can
Only be
Me.

Imperfect.

Sinner.

Seeking
Forgiveness.

Welcoming
Christ.

Waving
The white
Flag.

March 1st

Coming in
Like
A lion.

A wrecking
Ball
Of
Faith.

Ironing out
The tension.

Clearing
The blockages.

A miraculous
Delivery.

Rebirth.

You have
Suffered
Enough.

Now
Go make
Art.

Heal
Your
Tortured soul.

Show this
Wicked town
Something
Beautiful
And
New.

Perfect results.

Yielded
By
An imperfect
Process
Of Struggle
Anger
Worry
And stress.

Are omelets
Really worth
All
The broken
Eggs?

Only to
Those
Enjoying
The omelet.

He
Who has
The yolk
On
His fingers
Gets no
Sympathy.

Cage free
Fighting
Is
Barbaric.

No shame
In
Tapping
Out.

March 3rd

Turning
The page.

The long
Cycle
Comes to
An end.

A good time
To hit
The reset
Button.

Say goodbye to
The things
That
Must be
Left behind.

Strengthen
The things
That
Will
Remain.

The stage
Is
Set.

Take
Your place
At
The table.

March 4th

Shoveling
Out from under
The anger
And
Disappointment.

Old patterns
Resurface
But are
Kept in
Check.

Another test
Passed.

Flying
Color
Blind.

I am beginning
To get
Glimpses of
The joy
That comes in
Accepting
His will.

There is more
Where
That came
From.

March forth
And
Find it.

March 5th

A phat
Tuesday.

A last
Gasp
Of fight
From
The opposition.

The defenses
Prove
Solid.

Bending
But
Never breaking.

Just
A boy
With a new
Haircut.

And
A new
Path
Wide open
In front of
Me.

I will
Travel
At my own
Pace.

March 6th

Ashes
To
Ashes.

Another hero
Falls.

The beast
Adds
More kindle
To the fire.

Never
To be
Extinguished.

We will
March
On.

As
The fox
Chases
The deer.

The artist
Will soon
Be awakened

At the
Omega point.

Meet
The new
Moon.

Same as
The old
Moon.

You
Fool.

Burying
The hatchet.

Learning to
Hit
The target.

Marveling at
The magic.

But my heart
Lies
In a different
Castle.

Take
A toast
To what
Might have been.

If
Either of us
Knew
How to
Dance.

Stumbling.

Stepping
On
Toes.

Caught
Up in
The riptide.

Knocking
On
The door.

March 8th

You
Will not
Keep me
Zoned in.

My mission
Here
Is
Bigger.

Passing
The torch
To a new
Generation
Of heroes.

Fallen angels
Saying hello
From
The other side.

No news
Is
Good.

Do you
Remember
Who
I was?

Vestiges
Of
A Past
Life.

An interloper
In this
One.

My ghost
Has traveled
Far.

March 9th

Everybody loves
A parade.

Except
The war-weary
Heroes
In need of
Rest.

But
The show
Must
Go on.

Pomp
And
Circumstance.

Bread
And
Circuses.

Ashes
To
Ashes.

Dust
To
Dust.

In the shadow
Of
The churches
Who knows
What
They pray?

Line
The streets
For one
Last look
Because
I ain't
Marching
Anymore.

March 10th

Under
A coating
Of ice.

The depression
Returns.

A non-starter.

With
No friends
In sight.

Just
A past
They refuse to
Let go
Of.

While
You're alone
On the new shore.

Waiting
In vain.

Hurting.

Living
A life
No one
Is celebrating.

Just
Want to
Sleep.

March 11th

Paranoia.

Paranoia.

Everybody
Is out
To get you.

Just
Need
Some release.

And
Some sleep.

The rainbow
Soul
Is revealed.

Some praise.

Some mock.

Others
Are confused
By the sight.

Grown weary
By the leap
Forward.

Spirt week
Reveals
The spiritually
Weak.

Find
Comfort in
The Word.

March 12th

Good news!

The scans
Are
Clear.

No danger
In sight.

Your efforts
Have paid
Off.

God is
Good.

Time
To celebrate.

But
You are still
You.

Alone.

Chosen
By none.

Tolerated
By a few.

Untouched
And
Out of touch.

Waiting.

Biding time.

Break me
Out of
This prison.

I have lost
The keys.

March 13th

The same
Outlook
On life.

Just
Framed differently.

Making others
Green
With envy.

But
They would choke
On the cake
Before
Reaching
The icing.

Losing
Their breath.

Sprinting
To catch
Up.

In a race
I'm not
Running.

Just strolling
Through
A world
That
I refuse
To conform
To.

A crash course
In
Covering
A lot of
Ground.

Learning to
Trust is
The hardest
Part.

Still feel
The phantom itch
On
The severed limb
Of
My old
Life.

Just need
To stop
Scratching.

Put both
Hands on
The wheel
And
Drive forward.

As
More
Puzzle pieces
Fall
Into place.

March 15ᵗʰ

Beware
The ides.

Like
A shot
In
The face.

Knock
Some sense
Into you.

Wake
You up.

Get
Your priorities
Straight.

There will be
No relief.

Or celebration.

Just
Ebbs and flows
Of
Expectations.

So work
When it is time
To work.

Rest
When it is time
To rest.

And
When roses appear
Stop.

Smell them.

March 16th

A steady pace.

Not conforming
To
The pattern
Of
The race.

Listening
To
Inner guidance.

That's what
You need
To make a
Moon shot.

It's not just
Getting there.

It's also about
Coming back.

A period
Of
Black out.

And then
Splash
Down.

We've returned
To
Normalcy.

But
Will never be
The same
Again.

Youthful folly
Leading to
The source.

Four decades
Summed up
By
Three pennies.

The old bridges
Can be
Burned.

The rainbow
One
Awaits.

Don't forget to
Notice
The colors.

As you count
The stars
Signifying
Your future.

The snakes
Have been
Driven
Out.

Time
To breathe
Fire.

Because
Hope's
Alive.

March 18ᵗʰ

A restless night
Yields to
A calm day.

The train
Keeps chugging
Down the track
As
The conductor
Is nowhere
To be found.

Not all
Are aboard
But
They don't
Really have
A choice.

I seek
Sanctuary
In
The Word.

But it is hard
To escape
The roar
Of the war.

In time
I will
Achieve
My moment.

March 19ᵗʰ

Deeper down
The rabbit hole
Of faith.

You will
Find your joy
There.

After first
Achieving
Peace.

Don't be afraid
Of
Forgetting.

Your muscle
Memory is
Strong.

And
The heart is
The strongest
Muscle.

It will
Remember when
It's time
To play.

There is
No rust.

Game
Set
Now go
Find
Your match.

March 20th

Gagging
On the pill
Of negativity.

It has
No place
Inside of
You.

Spit
It all
Out.

Focus
On
Your growth.

Focus
On
Your path.

Shine
A light
To guide
You.

Others will
Follow
If they choose.

But
No looking
Back.

No going.
Back.

Avoid
The saltiness.

Temper
The sweetness.

Spring is here.

March 21st

The boat is
Fully
Out to sea.

The sight of
Those waving
From
The shore
Is sad
To see.

A cleansing rain
Comes.

Sure to wash
Away
The sticky residue
Of death.

Rest
Will be
Assured.

Renewal
Will
Come.

A tuned-up
Vehicle.

A gathering
Of saints
And sinners.

And those
In the middle of
The Venn diagram.

Lord
Have mercy
On
The mocker.

Polishing
A diamond
Is rough
Business.

There's an intensity
In her eyes.

A familiarity
As well.

Makes me want
To
Correct
My mistakes.

Is it
A glimpse of
My future?

Or just something
To lead me

Further
From my past?

I don't know
Anymore.

I just follow
Orders
To avoid
Chaos.

March 23rd

Nourishment.

The lost
Is now
Found.

It is safe
To return
To
The woods.

Just stay
On your path.

Following
Prophets
Instead of
Profits.

Poetry is
Found at
A slower pace.

Who are you
Racing against
Anyway?

There's no
Need to
Keep sharpening
Your sword.

Just plow ahead
Forward.

Surrender
Your king.

March 24th

As the week's
Work comes
To an end.

The depression
Creeps back
In.

Always waiting
In
The wings.

Not all
Horseshoes are
Lucky.

Some suck
The life
Out of you.

As fickle friends
Continue to
Forsake
You.

And family
Celebrates
In
Your absence.

Alone
Wallowing
In
Broken dreams.

March 25th

Focused
And
Determined.

Razor sharp.

Slicing stars
Out of
The white
Emptiness.

A master
Of
The blade.

But still
Light like
A feather.

Gently
Guided by
The soft breeze
Of God's will.

Offering
No resistance.

Go ahead
Make
My day.

And I did.

A time
To honor
The mother
Of us
All.

March 26th

The cycle of
Rest
And
Restlessness
Persists.

What
Will tonight
Bring?

Perhaps
An antidote
Is found.

Deep in
The frequency
Of sound.

Tones
To heal.

As waking
Life becomes
More dreamlike.

The slumber
Of familiar patterns
And
Routines.

And the same
People
Wearing
Many masks.

Will somebody
Open up
A window?

March 27th

Bombarded
By
A barrage
Of buzzwords.

Just another pill
That I will
Not swallow.

But
I guess
There is nothing
Called
A free lunch.

Only
The Word
Of
God is
Free.

Spiritual dryness
Quenched by
A liquid
Church.

Bathing
In the sounds
Of worship.

A prodigal son
Returning
For a visit.

But
It's not
My home.

March 28ᵗʰ

A deep
Belly
Breath.

As the wheel
In the sky
Keeps on
Turning.

Remaining
Mindful
By emptying
The mind.

Closing
The mouth.

Opening
The heart.

Sharing
Wisdom.

A family
Redeemed.

By
The new
Generation.

Breaking
The spell.

It's been
A long
Hard
Road.

But
There's always
Light.

A beautiful day
In
The neighborhood.

But when
You reach
New heights
All
The pulls
In your life
Appear
Downward.

Just need
To trust
The ebbs
And flows
Of the tides.

It's all in
Your head.

You will
Always be
A sheep
Among goats.

The wheat
In
The chaff.

Enjoy
The growth
Of spring.

There is still
Time before
Harvest.

March 30th

Lightning
Strikes
The tower.

The wake up
Call
Has been
Received.

The torch
Brings light
To the darkness.

The cards
Reveal
The present.

You still
Create
The future.

Don't plant
Seeds
In
Rocky soil.

Hold firm
To your beliefs.

And let
The good
Times
Roll.

March 31st

Tensions
Hangs over
A family
Reunion.

And
The beat
Goes on.

The world
Appears
More and more
Bitter.

As faith
Sweetens
The soul.

No more
Tolerance
Of the noise.

I just want
To bathe
In the music
And rest
In His
Silence.

Catch
The twenty-two.

You're on
The right
Track.

April 1ˢᵗ

Pictures
Of
The past.

People
We were
But really
Never were.

The arrow
Is not
The bow.

Any fool
Knows that.

The past
Never existed.

But
The mess
Still remains.

Move forward
By
Cleaning up.

Life
Has finally
Brought you
To
Your knees.

Thank God
For
That.

April 2nd

The wheel
In my mind
Keeps on
Sinning.

I don't know
What I'll do
With
My tomorrows.

Surrendering
Without
Retreating.

Moving forward
By
Letting go.

Time
To give
It up.

And
Find beauty
In
The breakdown.

Patiently humble.

Watching
The turmoil
Of beings.

With
A compassioned
Detachment.

April 3rd

I can only
Imagine.

What
My prime
Will
Feel like.

No longer
Bottled up.

Clouds
Have
Dissipated.

Demons
Boxed up.

Not letting this one
Go to
The judges.

As I live
My truth
With
More force.

I can
Speak it
More confidently.

Not about to
Blow
The long snap.

Game's on
The line.

April 4th

This is
Nowhere
Near my
Comfort zone.

Yet
I feel
Strangely
Comfortable

Wow
God is
Good.

Uplifting
An entire town
In one room.

Ain't nothing
Tricky
About that.

Paterson falls
But
Your tower
Of faith
Stands strong.

With a new
Birth
On the horizon.

His spirit
Is still
In there.

April 5th

A swollen temple.

No place
To worship.

Just
Untimely
Death fantasies.

Toys
That should have
Already been
Put away.

An overactive
Imagination.

Mixed with
The echoes
Of delusion.

All things
To account for
When defending
Your life.

Where
Good folks go
When
They die.

April 6th

Another glorious day
In His creation.

The line between
Prayer
And
Poetry
Begins
To blur.

The queen
Walks alone
But finds
Clarity
And closure.

The princess
Brings joy
To the stoic
Worshippers.

Family
Breaks bread
Together
As the battles
Rage on.

Terms of peace
Must be
Brought
To the table.

April 7th

Drawn into
Deep waters
By the enemy.

I couldn't
Resist
The currents.

So
I had to
Helplessly
Paddle.

With
Meaningless
Prattle.

We all have
So much more
To learn.

Resisting
The desire
For release.

But
I could use
A little
Comfort.

And
Joy.

Lord knows
It's not good
When
Man
Is
Alone.

April 8th

A labor
Of love.

The beauty of
A career.

Encapsulated in
A rectangle.

Hanging on
A wall.

I just had
A vision.

And
A stapler.

The angels
Did
The rest.

I couldn't
Always speak
Of the Father
And
The Son.

But
The Holy Spirit
Never left
My side.

A faithful
Friend.

Taken
For granted.

April 9th

A friendship
Reduced to
A letter.

A coda
To the
What could
Have beens.

The fabric
Is beginning
To be torn.

Beauty is
Revealed
But
Uncertainty
And
Anxiety
Rule
The day.

I stand
Alone.

Detached.

Observing
The parade.

A scene
I'm all
Too familiar with.

This is not
My first
Rodeo.

April 10ᵗʰ

Heat
Rushes to
The head.

But
The fire
In
The stomach
Is kept
At bay.

It's an ugly
Business
Run by
Small men.

And I
Just
Want to
Rise above
It all.

Lord
Show me
The way.

Am I
Your warrior?

Or learning
To yield?

Should I
Bring fire?

Or swim in
A new pond?

The questions come
Too quick
To process.

April 11th

The divine
Sense of
Humor.

All
Part of
The Ma and Pa
Method.

Is
The Holy Spirit
Just
Teasing me
Again?

Or
Will there
Be
Actualization?

A chance
Encounter.

Shows
We're all
Moving
Forward.

A student
Approaches
The teacher.

Patience is
Tested.

The smile
Of Jesus.

The bonus
Tracks
Of Heaven.

April 12th

What a difference
A day
Makes.

Ideas are
Fleeting.

The Word is
What
Endures.

A cleansing
Rain comes
As night
Falls.

I will not let
The ship
Go down.

But
I may jump
At the first
Sight of
Safe harbor.

A legacy
Destined
To be packed
Away in
A plastic bin.

Enjoy it
While
It's here.

April 13th

Breakfast
With champions.

Dinner
With royalty.

Hills climbed.

On
Damp
Lakeside
Roads.

As the fog
Lifts.

And
The sun
Rises.

There is
Still
Work
To be
Done.

But
The garden
Is restored.

Raise
The flag.

The fights
Are over.

No longer
Worth
The price of
Admission.

A lonely tree.

Watching
Over
The turmoil
Of creation.

Opportunities
Missed.

The tiger
Returns
From hiding.

Balance is
Restored
As
Redemption is
Mastered.

The fast
Has been
Broken.

Call in
The knights
And
Freemasons.

Heaven
Has been
Scouted.

And there
Lies still
A lonely tree.

April 15th

The cathedral
Crumbles.

A lesson
In
Impermanence.

Only
The spirit within
Endures.

Fight
To save it.

Kindle
Its fire.

Let it
Burn you.

Like
The anger
Within.

Polluting
Your mind.

The plank
In your eye.

Still
Blinding you
Of
The present.

Stuck in
The past.

A change
In titles.

But
The same
Old you.

Youthful
Folly is
Behind me.

The well
Has been
Renewed.

And
Restored.

While
The Buddha
Gets a new
Coat
And
Crown.

The purple
Chakra
Is splattered
Everywhere.

As peace
On Earth
Squeals
Through the
Ear buds.

What
A glorious
Run.

Through
The hill
Country.

Back to
The source.

April 17th

This is
Not
My family.

I am
Just
An interloper.

A believer
Following
Orders.

Keeping
Promises.

Paying
The price
For my sins.

What was
Freely given
Can be
Taken
Without recompense.

Look it up.

It doesn't end
Like this.

The preacher
Knows
The score.

As
My body
Lies
Tired
And sore.

A cross
Of gold.

Imbued with
The Holy Spirit.

After
The long journey
Down from
The top
Of the world.

Tired feet
In need of
A bath.

A divinely ordained
Birthday
Present for
A saint.

As the blur
Of the
Squeezed apple
Fills
The train's window.

Give it all
To me
Life.

Pleasure me
As I
Pleasure you.

April 19th

It took some
Amazing
Grace.

To get
Me
Over
That hill.

But
This wretch
Did it.

It's the least
I can
Do.

For He
Who carried
The cross
For me.

On this
Good
Friday.

The fortress
Of faith
Has been
Solidified.

Ready
To withstand
Any onslaught.

Foreign
Or
Domestic.

It's finally
Safe
To go
Back in
The water.

April 20th

A soft
Reset.

A mountain
Of accomplishment
Behind you.

Endless work
Ahead of
You.

It
Will never
Be enough.

Just enjoy
The beauty of
The moment.

That's all
We will
Ever have.

Experiences.

Not
Outcomes.

Appreciation.

Not
Expectations.

It's time
To
Go.

April 21st

Rejoice!

He
Has
Risen!

Greeted by
The deer
Before
The sun
Wakes for
The day.

The final
Test
Passed.

A celebration
Earned.

The somber
Season of
Sacrifice
Succumbs to
The renewal
And hope
Of spring.

Joy
Returns to
The church.

As
The blessing
Is
Received.

You are
Appreciated.

April 22nd

A home
Leaving
And
A home
Coming.

Neither one
Triumphant.

Quietly
In the middle of
Different
Dramas
And agendas
And expectations.

None of them
Serve me.

So
I just
Watch.

Detached.

Allow
The current
To move
Me.

But not
Be moved
By it.

Toes up.

Not getting
Caught.

Supple
But
Firm.

April 23rd

A family
Fracturing.

Blood
Washed away by
The waters
Of life.

Functional disagreement
In
Close proximity
Is
Pain.

So
Better to
Keep at
A distance.

Embracing
The Earth
Changes
Heralded by
The youth.

Seeking
The greatest
Love.

Appearing
Indifferent.

Because
I care
Too much.

There are
No maps
For
These territories.

April 24th

I don't know
Who I am
Anymore.

But
I love him
Deeply.

Acceptance
Has been
Bequeathed to
Me
Through
God's will.

The ego's been
Reduced to
A puppet
With
The Holy Spirit
Pulling
The strings.

Tethered to
The past.

Thanks to
Some
Brotherly love.

As the music
Of new
Memories
Is heard
From
My window.

April 25th

The puzzle
Has been
Solved.

Each piece
Found
Its place.

Now
Each place
Seeks
Its peace.

As
The turmoil
Of beings
Grows
Deafening.

And
The distant shore
Of return
Gets lost
On
The horizon.

I calmly
Paddle
My boat
Named
Faith.

Following
Jesus
Who strides ahead
Of me.

He knows
The Way.

But warns
There are
No
Shortcuts.

April 26th

Winning
Loses
Its meaning
When
Nobody is
Keeping score.

Towing
The line
Between
Competition
And chaos.

Is it
In
Or
Is it
Out?

Is this
Work
Or
Is this
Play?

The beauty of
The breakdown.

Where
Genius finds
Its courage.

And rain
Washes
The slate
Clean.

As
The once
Solid ground
Turns
Muddy.

But still
You dig.

April 27th

Brought back
From
The dead.

Alone
In
An empty theater.

Walking
Among
The crowded aisles
Of
Emptiness.

Picking apart
The scant remains
Of
The corpse.

This is
What an end
Of
An era
Looks like.

To most
It is hopelessness
And despair.

To the prophet
It is
The seed
Of rebirth
And renewal.

The breakthrough
Has
Arrived.

The purr
Of a cat
Vibrates
On my chest.

Soothing
A heart
That's been
Working
Overtime.

There's
No rest
For
The wicked.

And
Even less
For
The servants
Of God.

So
Hold
Your purple lights
Up high.

Keep
Waging hope
In
The wilderness.

The gift
Has been
Delivered.

Rejoice
And
Be glad.

April 29th

The honeymoon
With Christ
Comes to
An end.

Now
We must
Endure
The ups
And downs
Of building
A life
Together.

While
Depression takes
Every opportunity
To come
Out of
The shadows.

Reminding you
Of all
You lack.

And the friends
And family
Who
Forsake you.

I never felt
More alone
Than
Right now.

A course
Correction.

Brings me
Closer to
The resurrection.

Living
A life
That only
Makes sense
Because
God is
Real.

Eighty years
Of comfort
Is folly.

Next to
The promise
Of eternity.

Your bus
Is going
Nowhere
If
That won't
Jump start
You.

You'll be alone
On
Your island.

Never
Seeing green
Pastures.

May 1st

A new life
Rushes
Into
The world.

In a hurry
To unleash all
The hope
Joy
And redemption
That
She promises.

Meanwhile.

A mother
And son
Deal with
The exfoliation
Of feelings.

Stumbling
Through
What emerges
On
The surface.

But still
Better than
Pushing
It all
Back down.

Nobody
Said it
Would
Be easy.

May 2nd

Not nervous.

Not excited.

Just
Another day
At
The office.

The thrill
Is
Gone.

Either
My heart is
No longer
In it.

Or
My heart is
Too numb
To be
In anything
Anymore.

At least
I have
This.

The common
Thread in
The chaotic
Fabric being
Weaved.

A tapestry
Of
Uncertainty.

May 3rd

The morning
After
Triumph.

Too tired
To enjoy
The spoils
Of victory.

Resting
Atop
The new plateau.

Looking up
At
The new heights.

It promises
To take you.

But
Right now
Enjoying
The view
Is enough.

The next
Stage
Is not
A hazardous climb.

Just
A slow
March.

To
The beat
Of
God's drum.

May 4th

A tangled web
Is being
Weaved.

And we
Already killed
The messenger.

Inspection
Passed
With ease.

So
The journey
Can continue
In earnest.

Accepting
The world
More
And more.

As I
Increasingly
Detach
From it.

Eat
Drink
Work the body
Honor God
Study
Write
And
Serve.

May 5th

There was
No stopping
The waste
From
Coming out.

So
You might
As well
Expediate
The process.

Hopefully
I won't have
To do that
Again.

These
Hard resets
Are becoming
Harder.

But
Each one
Brings me
Closer to
The future

And
Further away
From
The past.

I know
What direction
I should
Go.

The thrill
Is
Gone.

Going through
The motions
While remaining
Emotionless.

I need
To find
A new well
To draw
From.

The party
Is over.

And
I have
Overstayed
My welcome.

All
That remains
To comfort me
Is
The Word.

I bathe
In it
To prevent
The filth
From
Sticking.

It
Showers me
With
Joy.

May 7th

Unashamed.

Of how
I feel.

Of what
I believe.

Of who
I am.

Unashamed.

Because of
His love.

Because of
His grace.

Because of
His mercy.

Unashamed.

Nothing
Without Him.

Everything
Because of
Him.

Thank you
God.

Thank you
Jesus.

Thank you
Holy Spirit.

Use me
As you wish.

May 8th

Like water
Spilled on
The ground.

This day
Could have
Gone
In many
Different directions.

My mind
Could have
Taken me
One way.

My pride
Could have
Taken me
Another.

Who knows where
My heart
Could have
Lead me.

But
It was God
Who
Got me
Here.

Allow me
To never be
Recovered from
Your grace.

May 9th

Sometimes
I don't know
What
I'm feeling
Anymore.

But
"In control"
Is
Definitely not
One of
The options.

And neither is
"Happy".

I pray for
A way out.

But
I see none.

I feel
Rejected.

Discarded.

Tolerated.

But
Not loved.

Alone.

Alone
In my head.

Alone
In my heart.

This is what
God wills
For
His disciples.

The sun
Will come
Out
Tomorrow.

The stepson
Will run
Tomorrow.

In his
Honor.

But
Today
I relish
The small victories.

Looking up
After
Trending down.

Slowly
Chipping away
At stone.

The tunnel
Begins to
Take shape.

Still
A long way
From
The light.

But soon
There will be
Space
Enough
For others
To follow.

May 11ᵗʰ

Right
Down to
The wire.

But
Edged out
At the end.

Just
More motivation
To keep
Training.

Preparing for
What lies
Ahead.

As
The sands
Shift
Below us.

Family
Friends
And neighbors.

Hold
Onto
Each other.

There is
A core
That is
Not rotten.

A fruit
That will
Not spoil.

Eat
From the tree
Where
Your roots
Lie.

May 12th

A tale of
Two churches.

One
Timely.

The other
Timeless.

One
Casting
A wide net.

The other
Pointing
The way through
The narrow gate.

One
Fresh and hip.

The other
Aged and elegant.

Both
Putting on
A show.

Music.

Pageantry.

Message.

Drama.

But
No escape from
Reality.

Just
A truth
That's real.

May 13th

A cold
November's rain.

Deep in
The heart
Of May.

It is
Taking longer
For people
To warm
Up.

Carrying
A basket full
Of health.

Bolstered by
Positive habits
And routines.

It will
Get me
Through all
Climates.

Time to
Loosen
The reins

Remove
The blinders.

And
Stride on.

May 14th

The military.

The industrial.

The complex.

Maintenance
Is required.

It will
Get done.

A piece of
Cake.

It this
A simulation?

Or
Is this
Real life?

What's
The difference?

When you're trying
To win
The game.

I still
Chop wood.

I still
Carry water.

But
I ain't
Marching.

And
I ain't
Playing.

Not anymore.

May 15th

A beast
Stalks.

Bringing fear
To the hearts
Of the weary.

But
It cannot spoil
The birthday
Celebration of
Our fallen hero.

As those
Who marched
With him
Gather
And rejoice.

We will not be
Beaten.

The struggle
Will
Go on.

While
New troops
Are called to
The front.

May 16ᵗʰ

Never
A dull moment.

Always
A new twist
In
The drama.

Satan stirs
The pot
In
The city
Of brotherly turmoil.

Condescension
Spills over
As the roots
Are obscured by
The thick broth
Of denial.

But
It's no soup.

Just
Nuts.

A strange game.

The only
Winning move
Is not
To play.

Towing
The line between
Tired
And
Exhausted.

As subtle as
The difference between
Weather
And
Climate.

It this
A tough day
Or
A long season?

The moon is
Full.

Can
You say
The same
Of
Your heart?

The cacophony
Of
A child's play
Definitely
Warms it.

And
Brings it
Joy.

But
The filter
Needs
Adjusting.

May 18th

So humbling
To be
In the presence of
Trees.

Giants
Of patience
Perseverance
And fortitude.

My concerns
And pursuits
Are folly
To them.

They would
Drop them
From their branches
At the lightest
Breeze.

Leaving
No mark
To ring true
In their barks.

Like ripples
In a pond
Whose nature is
To be
Still.

May 19th

The struggle
To stay above
Water is
Unceasing.

Drop
My guard
For a second
And
The blows
Come from
All angles.

It's tough
Squeezing through
The eye
Of the needle.

And
I'm not
A rich man.

The delayed delivery
Of relief
Frustrates.

As I work
Way too hard
For second best.

But
This is how
I fight
My battles.

May 20th

A brave
New world.

For
A stubborn
Old soul.

Defender of
The straight
Black line.

Denying access
Down the
Slippery slope.

What
Will come
Of him?

As life becomes
Far stranger than
Any fiction.

He has
Picked
A side.

Must he
Hide?

Or take
A bold stand?

Or
Will they
Let him
Live
His peace?

May 21st

The release of
Emotional baggage
Over plates of
Fermented cabbage.

Friends
Reunited.

Brothers
Of the road.

Enlightened
Rouges.

A well
Earned
Recess.

After
A long
Day of
Hard lessons.

And
Only electives
Left to
Take.

Life is
Good.

When
You are
The property
Of angels.

May 22nd

We will
Look back at
These
As
The salad days.

Whatever
That means.

The days of
The gambler's
Big winning
Streak.

As
The house
Endured
The illness.

The days when
Things were
So simple
And orderly.

In all
Their complex
Chaos.

Before
We were all
In on the joke.

And realized
Absurdity
Is meant
To be
Relished.

May 23rd

Sometimes
You have to
Let
The devil
Back in you.

To
Remind you
How weak
You are.

The king
Maker.

Master of
The vibes.

And
I cannot
Serve
Two masters.

So
I must
Put one
Up on
The shelf.

As I
Commit to
The path
That denies
The self.

Let
My will
Be
Your perfect will
Oh Lord!

May 24th

Back up
From
Rock bottom.

Each time
The climb
Is not as
High.

But
The shame
Cuts
Deeper.

You should
Know better.

The devils
That caused you
To surrender
Will
Always be
Stronger than
You.

Don't let pride
Tell you
Otherwise.

Seek
Your pleasure
Only in
The process.

Escape
Like resistance
Is futile.

May 25th

Seeking
Peace.

And knowing
Where to
Find it.

Just lacking
Time.

Hoping for
Joy.

Grasping at
Straws.

As it remains
Concealed.

Expecting
Competence.

Finding
Disappointment.

Prepared
To fold
My hand
In frustration.

I'm running
Out of
Cards
To play.

And
Long weary
For
A new deal.

May 26th

A day
Of diversions.

But
The unease
Remains
Lurking
In the background.

Old friends.
Reunite.

At home
But merely
Spectators.

In a world
That does not belong
To them.

They wouldn't want it
If
It was given.

The dissonance
Is exhausting.

No need to
Pick up
The phone.

Connection
Is
Lost.

May 27th

When
A celebration
Becomes
A stale formality
You know
The enemy
Has
Its teeth
Sunk in.

You made
A sacrifice
On the altar
Of
No self-discipline.

Only to be
Anointed by
The deacon
Of
Self-righteous rage.

You already
Played out
All your moves.

And remain
Cornered by
Bishops.

A helpless pawn
Among
Kings.

May 28th

Suicidal
Ideations.

Always
Lingering in
The dark recesses
Of your
Tainted mind.

Ready to
Fill
The vacuum
Created by
Your sins.

This
Is
No
Joke.

This
Is
No
Game.

This is
Nature
At
Its worst.

A hailstorm
Of hell
Bringing
Darkness.

Only
The promise of
A newborn's smile
Can preserve
The light
And bring
Power
Back to
A lost soul.

May 29th

Like a bat
Out of Hell.

Feelings
Long brewing
Spill over
In
Hot anger.

Meaning is
Lost.

Understanding
Obscured.

Shame
And frustration
Win
The day.

Makes everything
That came
Before it
Seem
Fraudulent.

Makes everything
That comes
After it
Seem like
A charade.

Regrets.

I've had
A few.

May 30ᵗʰ

He has
Ascended.

Opening
The door of
Our destiny.

Stop looking
Up.

Just start
Following.

Help others
On the path.

But
Untie
All ropes.

And
Pull up
The anchor.

Allow nothing
To keep you
Down.

The waters
May be
Rough.

The crew
May be
Getting restless.

But
The shore
Isn't as distant
As it seems.

Ice
Fills
The veins
As
His focus
Sharpens.

A pastoral setting
Hosts
The youthful warriors
Of spring.

The balance
Teeters
Back
And forth
Until
Our hero
Achieves
Equilibrium.

You've definitely seen
Some things
That can't go
Unseen.

With eyes
That are both
Gentle
And
Rugged.

June 1st

A page
Has been
Turned.

Hills
Climbed.

Spirits
Uplifted.

But
We've been
Pulled down
From here
Again
And again.

So
Forgive
My weariness.

I can
Throw punches.

But
I'm always
Dropping
My guard.

Leaving myself
Open.

Leaving myself
Vulnerable.

Instead of
One united
I am
A house
Divided.

And that
I cannot
Stand.

June 2nd

The holy man
Says farewell to
The town
Who raised him
Up.

The saint of
Lost causes
Smiles
As the desperate
Grows brave.

While the gypsy
Gets a peak
Behind the curtain
And sees
The sickness
And depravity.

This is not
Your home.

She is not
Your mother.

Just
Another cross
To bear.

June 3rd

Riding
The ups
And downs.

Making
A splash.

The new moon
Is
A harbinger of
Good times
To come.

You have yet
To find
Your tribe
But
You're finding
Your peace.

And
You know
Your place.

All else
Will come through
Acceptance.

Trust God.

Carry
Your crosses
Joyfully.

And stop
Fighting demons
Where
They don't exist.

June 4th

I voted.

I picked
A side.

I didn't
Waver.

Sometimes
Simply participating
Is taking
A bold stand.

Against
The apathetic.

Against
The cynics.

Against
The non-believers.

Against
Those
Who think
The walls
Are crumbling.

As they
Thoughtlessly toss
The bathwater
I cradle
The baby.

Nurturing
The torch
That holds back
The darkness.

June 5th

The day after
The hard part.

Keeping score
In a competition
Of formalities.

The cycle
Keeps
Returning to
The same spot.

As
The groove
Deepens
And
The needle
Wears thin.

The saint
Sends messages
From beyond
The grave.

But I remain
Unmoved.

Detached.

Lost
To the world.

But found
By the Word.

Amen.

June 6th

I get knocked down
But
I get up
Again.

The cold
Unrelenting
Ocean
Will never
Keep me
Down.

It will
Always be
Stronger than
Me.

But I cannot
Lose
If
I keep
Fighting it.

A beach invasion.

To liberate
The allies.

Rescue them
From the clutches
Of evil.

Don't lose
Hope.

We're coming
For you.

June 7th

The life
You live
Is
The lesson
You teach.

So
I'm trying
To leave behind
A curriculum's worth
Of memories
And examples.

But
All I got
Are
Some photographs.

A slideshow
Of moments
Where
The meaning
Is lost.

Unfiltered
But not
Unobscured.

A library of
Yearbooks
Devoid of
Signatures.

June 8th

A day
Of fights.

As
The young knight
Emerges
Victorious
Against
His old rival.

Withstanding
The volleys
Of life
With
The precision
And determination
Of
A destined champion.

And
A glimmer
Of hope
Emerges
On
The horizon.

As angels
Conspire
To fill
The missing piece
Of
The puzzle.

June 9th

There is
No moderation
In me.

No
Middle way.

I can't have
My cake
And eat it
Too.

So
I must
Commit to
The way
Of truth.

The only spirit
I accept
Is
The spirit
That is
Holy.

The anonymous advocate
Pulling all
My strings.

The only sweetness
I want
Is
The sweetness
Of you.

My boyhood toys
Have been
Tossed.

I'm ready
To be
Your man.

June 10th

Pushing
The body.

Calming
The soul.

Feeding
The mind.

The countdown
Clock
Keeps ticking.

A finale
Is
Inevitable.

The end
Reminds you of
The dashed hopes
Of the beginning.

While
Bringing up
The bitterness
Of the middle.

Throughout
It all
You were
Alone.

So
Who better
To celebrate with
Now that
It's done.

June 11th

Doubling down
On
Double sessions.

Laying the foundation
For what's
To come.

Living in
The future.

While tying up
The loose ends
Of the past.

Your finish
Is strong.

Your new beginning
Is even
Stronger.

Stay
Above it
All.

Let
The drama
Play out
As it must.

A long hauler
Pays
No mind
To
The fleeting
Parade
Of the day.

June 12th

Throwing roses
In
The lake.

The icing
On
The cake.

A birthday
And
An anniversary.

Recounting horrors
Of
The past.

A monster
In
The woods.

An evil
We can't
Deny.

Lurking
Within us
All.

As
We point
Desperately
At
The moon.

With fingers
Broken
Beyond repair.

June 13ᵗʰ

The penultimate
Day.

Feelings reign
Inside.

As
The house
Prepares
To be
Cleaned.

You are
What endures.

Beyond
The pomp
And circumstance.

A legacy
Of learning.

Growing
Beyond
All limits.

You saw it
Be put
Together.

You won't
Let them
Take it
Apart
Through
The arrogance
Of mediocrity.

June 14ᵗʰ

To be
So disconnected
Yet
The center
Of it all.

Plenty of
Loved ones
But
Not a friend
In sight.

Abandoned
By those
You helped
Lift up.

Without
A goodbye.

The air
Slowly escapes
The balloon
Of hope.

Will
I ever
Allow it
To be inflated
Again?

Seeking life
While still
Only
Bringing out
The dead.

June 15th

A gold medal day.

Seeds planted
In winter
Coming to
Full flower.

Validation
For sticking to
A path
Riddled
With thorns.

Confirmation
Of a future
Layered
With joy
And revelation.

Expectations
Tempered
But
Hope renewed.

Rooted in
The now.

Embracing
The process.

Let
The scroll
Continue
To unravel
Slowly.

June 16th

A pilgrim's
Progress.

In fits
And starts.

Back down
The valley
After climbing
Another
Mountain.

Leaving
More behind
As
The gate
Gets
Narrower
And Narrower.

Soon
There will be
Nothing left.

But
Isn't that
The point?

Emptying
The vessel
So
It can only
Be filled
By God.

Master
The body.

And
The heart
And mind
Will have
No choice
But
To fall
In line.

Even though
The spirits
Protect you.

Look
Both ways
Before
Crossing to
The next dimension.

Add some
More weight.

Your soul
Will not
Be crushed.

A saint
That's a sight
For
Sore eyes.

June 18th

God reigns.

While
An infant
Teaches
Her lessons.

And
A youth
Shares
Her wisdom.

Shining light
On
The folly
Of experience.

You dig into
Your trenches
Deeper.

Hoping
It gives you
The security
To share
Your love.

To find
Your satisfaction.

To seek
Your joy.

In Jesus
Christ alone.

Inspecting
The deck.

But
I never asked
To be
Dealt in.

Just
An anthropologist
Of
Organizational dynamics.

A reader
Of rooms.

A well-intentioned
Cohesion
Of some good
People.

Struggling
To keep
Their demons
Hidden.

As I lurk
On the fringes.

A reluctant
Volunteer.

June 20th

Look up
Child.

The Holy Mother
Has you
On
Your knees.

As you
Light
A candle
For
The teacher
Of teachers.

And
Are led
Away from
Temptation.

Into
An island
Of paradise.

Of passion
Fruit
And hibiscus.

You retire
To
Your pod.

Thinking
A day
Couldn't be
Any more
Complete.

June 21st

Among
An endless parade
Of humanity.

Lost in
The vapors
Of reality.

A student
And
A teacher
Find each other.

Sharing in
The good news.

While
The chessmen
And gypsies
Remain
Oblivious.

To
The portrait
Being drawn.

To
Those shouting
From
The rooftop.

This
Does have
A happy
Ending.

June 22nd

Awake in
One state.

Go to sleep
In another.

The cruel
Come down
Of returning
From a
Soul-expanding
Trip.

The long process
Of integration
Has only
Just begun.

The faint feeling
In your head
Is not
Chemically induced.

It's the feeling
Of being
Home.

Ain't nothing
Sweet
About it.

There's work
To be done
Here.

June 23rd

A gathering
Of heroes.

To remember
And fight
On.

A thousand stories
Told.

All with
The same
Ending.

Unified
In grief.

A solidarity
Of sadness.

Waging hope
Against
The windmills.

Living
The impossible
Dream.

Waking up
In
The swamp land.

Trying to
Pull
The drain.

June 24th

Rallying
The troops.

With
A storm
Of statistics.

All signs
Pointing to
Progress.

Yet
Despair
Still fills
The room.

While
The believers
Meet
In private.

To discuss
The life
To come.

The battle plans
Are taught.

As
The lieutenant
Shows
Her might.

It's the eve
Of
The invasion.

Woe to those
Who oppose
The light.

June 25th

Charging up
The hill.

Armed with
Grit
And
Raw emotion.

Eyes
Washed with
Tears.

See
The clarity
Of truth.

As
The children
Find
Their voice.

And
The men
Know when
To yield.

The future
Remains
Uncertain.

Though
The Word
Endures
Through time.

The ending
Of a chapter
In a book
Not yet
Begun.

June 26th

The suite
Life.

A spacious
Wonderland.

King-size
Comfort.

And
A royal feast.

We have it
Made in
The shade.

Protected
From
The cruel sun.

Proudly displaying
God's Son.

Worthless metal
But
Priceless meaning.

Drawing borders
With
Thick lines.

So
Don't cross them.

June 27ᵗʰ

A victorious
Last stand
In the heat.

The family
Of God
Will always
Prevail.

This is how
We fight
Our battles.

Shaking off
Death
Like
A rattle.

In a world
That's over-crowded
And
Over-commercialized.

There's only
One way
Around it.

And
You found it.

By grace.

By love.

By faith.

I am
No longer
A thief.

But
I still
Find occasion
To cheat.

It makes me
Adhere to
The rules
More
Strictly.

Stretching
The limits
Makes you
Remember why
You put them there
To begin with.

Discipline
Equals
Freedom.

Keep
That equation
Balanced
And
Life is
Grand.

Paying the price
For inviting
The dark arts
Into
My life.

As
The prophecy
Expires.

But
Not before
Overstaying
Its welcome.

And
Dashing hopes.

Thank you
God
For turning
My sin
Into
Strength.

My failure
Into
Fortitude.

My despair
Into
Deliverance.

Lead me
Through the
Narrow gate.

Allow me
In your
Celestial city.

June 30th

There's no rest
For progress.

As we try
To remember
The words of
The lost
Hymns of peace.

And give
Them back
To a world
Who forgot.

Redemption
Songs.

Running against
The wind.

Parched lips.

Ready
To stop
Before
The halfway mark.

But
Kept pushing.

Didn't
Look back.

Bore my cross
To
The end.

The least
I could
Do.

July 1st

Enjoy
The view
From
The throne
While
It still
Lasts.

Because
A younger
Version
Of yourself
Is ready
To defeat
You.

Setting
A new
Jazz standard.

Honoring
The past
While
Staking claims on
The future.

Leaving you
With nothing
But
The present.

Sitting on
The bench.

Just
An ordinary
Fellow
Who has
Completed
His work.

July 2nd

An arena
Filled
With grace.

Sold
Out for
Salvation.

Chanting
The name
Of Jesus.

The lyrics
Of love
Reverberating
Off
The ceiling.

While outside
The needy
Still need.

The broke
Are still
Broken.

The forsaken
Still
Forsake him.

People
United
In their sin.

Dancing
The dance
Of the lost.

Physical contact.

The gentle
Healing purr
On the heart.

Comfort.

Security.

A sugar rush
To the head.

At
Any moment
The bomb
May
Go off.

Mutually
Assured
Frustration.

Only through
The lens
Of tomorrows
Can we tell
A slip
From
A slide
From
A fall.

But today
We know
The will
Is
Weakening.

July 4th

Freedom
Is not
A piece
Of cake.

Everybody has
Their hang ups.

So
Not everybody
Can hang.

Just remain
In God.

In Jesus.

In the Holy Spirit.

And
Your fortress
Will be
Impenetrable.

From judgements.

From opinions.

From accusations.

From all
Circumstances
Beyond
Your control.

The true
Meaning
Of freedom.

July 5th

It is hard
To control
The heat
Without
Turning
Cold.

Exchange
Anger
For
Apathy.

Engagement
For
Escape.

We cannot
Live
In peace.

So
I must
Learn
The way
Of the sword.

Divide
And conquer

Those standing
Between you
And
The one
True way.

Overcome
The world.

July 6th

A hopeless sinner.

Falling short
Of
The glory
Of God.

Just trying
To do
The best
I can.

Making
Strides.

Making
Progress.

I can
Do this
All
Through Him
Who
Gives me
Strength.

Even in
My moments
Of weakness.

There is
Hope
On
The horizon.

Once
I navigate
Through
The jungle.

July 7th

The seventh day.

Rest.

Rest
In the love
Of God.

Rest
In the faith
You
Fought for
And won.

Rest
In the grace
That will
Always
Guide you.

Rest
Atop
The mountains
You climbed.

Rest
Atop
The wisdom
You earned.

Rest
Knowing that
You are
Protected.

Rest
Knowing that
You are
Complete.

Rest.

It is good.

July 8th

Rain leaves
The soil
Damp
And
Fertile.

A good time
To plant
A seed.

So
I reach out
To you
From
My secret
Place.

Creating
A rock bottom
To be
Rescued from.

Knowing all
Along
I have
Already
Been saved.

Knowing all
Along
I have
Never
Been alone.

Knowing all
Along
This is
My path.

July 9th

First contact.

Hope for
Life.

But
The signal
Is distant.

And of a
Different
Frequency.

Not yet
Sure if
Tuning to it
Will be
Possible.

Not quite
Sure if
I even
Want this.

Just want
A definitive
Path.

I abandoned
Limbo
For good.

Already bought
The ticket.

Up to you
If
You want
To come
Along for
The ride.

July 10th

An achingly
Slow
Rhythm.

Playing
Faintly in
The background.

Not distinct
Enough to
Dance to.

But
Just present
Enough to
Disrupt you
From
The music
Of
Your life.

Right now.

From hope
To novelty
To boredom
To abandon.

Too old
For games.

Yet
Too young
To stop
Playing.

July 11th

Detached.

Distant.

Difficult
To engage
With
The flotsam
And jetsam
Of life.

Have I
Gone in
Too deep?

Unwilling
And unable
To return
To surface.

Holding
My breath
As I
Sacrifice
The breadth
Of
My awareness.

Grasping hands
With
My savior.

Following
To a new
Shore
On
The horizon.

July 12th

Delayed
Gratification.

Better
To be stuck
In traffic
Than in
The accident
Causing
The traffic.

Still looking
For
Your center
Of gravity.

You have
All
The pieces.

But
No one
Is giving
You
The chance
To put them
Together.

Their dismissal
Of you
Is puzzling.

Retreat
Before
Escape
Is impossible.

July 13th

One hope dims
As another
Brightens.

A dance
Of shadows
On the cave walls
Of solitude.

Entertaining
But not
The truth.

It can't be
An early stoppage
If
The fight
Had yet
To begin.

There was
No bell.

Just
A lot of
Whistles.

No music.

Just noise.

July 14th

Confronting
The texts
Of terror.

The raw
Reality
Behind
The revelation.

Burning
The anger
In order
To enlighten
The joy.

Accepting
The futility
Of sugar coating
The brutality
Of honesty.

You are
Not
Penned in.

You have
Options.

You were
Set free.

Reject
The yoke
Of slavery.

July 15th

Paralyzed
In this
Holding cell
I created.

A stranger
To these
Strange times.

Disgusted by
The vanity
Of it all.

Rejecting
A world
That rejected
Me
For too long.

Invisible
To all
Except
The God
Who sees.

Who provides
For all
My needs.

By denying me
Of my wants.

No comfort.

No joy.

No peace.

July 16th

Putting in
The work.

Pounding
The pavement.

Creating
Distance.

Leaving
The past
Behind
Without
Abandoning it.

Just going
Forward.

Touched by
The Holy Spirit.

Who continues
To bestow you
With gifts.

And trust you
With jewels.

Use them
Well.

Because
You don't
Deserve
Them.

No one
Does.

Success
Sometimes comes
From falling
Short
Of your goals.

You wanted
So much
More.

But
You are still
In a
Really good
Place.

Hunger
Is good.

As long
As you
Don't get
Consumed by
Your appetites.

The full moon
Wanes.

During
A cleansing
Rain.

While
The heat
Is still
To come.

July 18th

Gaining traction.

But
There's still
Some mud
Left on
Your tires.

Hose 'em down
Before
You dirty up
Some places.

Putting in
Work.

But
There's still
A whole
Lot more
To do.

Good thing
You enjoy it.

Hitting
Your flow
State.

Creating
And building.

An architect
And
An artist.

July 19th

Routines.

Momentum.

Grooves.

Long-term
Decisions
Beginning
To pay
Dividends.

Compound
The interest.

Relish
The waiting.

Relish
The hard parts.

Enjoy
Eating the cake
Before
You even
Get to
The icing.

Chop
That wood.

Carry
That water.

Chop wood.

Carry water.

Chop.

Carry.

200

July 20th

Climbed
The mountain.

Went through
The portal.

Only
To find
More disappointment
On
The other
Side.

The life
Of the stomach
Is a dead end
Path.

The life
Of the crown
Leads to
Delusions
And disillusionment.

You have
No roots.

The fires
Of
The sacral
Must
Be used
To waken
The heart.

A hopeless sinner.

Falling short
Of the glory
Of God.

Trying
To finish
The race.

But stumbling
Over
Every hurdle.

A humbling
Place.

Where
Self-righteousness
Turns to
Shame.

Asking
For mercy.

And saved
Only by
His grace.

You
Are
Forgiven.

An attempt
To quiet
The noise.

The iron will
Has become
Rusty.

Only
The golden
Silence can
Reinforce it.

Retreat
Back to
Your core.

The heat
Will be
Washed
Away.

Like
The cleansing
Sweat
Dripping
From
Your face.

As you
Bow
Prostrate
On the mat.

Worshipping
The process.

July 23rd

Sweating
It out.

But still
Hitting
Milestones.

Finding
Simple
But elegant
Solutions.

To
The most
Complex
Problems.

By just
Going
Forward.

In spite of
Myself.

Battle
Tested.

Nothing new.

A war
Of
Attrition.

As
The devils
Keep falling
Around me.

I stay
Standing.

Anger
Begets
More anger.

Healing
The world
Is
An inside job.

And sometimes
You have
To go
Outside
To get that
Perspective.

To see
The sickness.

To feel
The anger.

To turn
Away
From it.

Knowing Christ
Is
The only
Way.

The only
Path
To peace.

July 25th

A return
To normalcy.

But
The new
Normal
Is certainly
More new
Than normal.

Running
Through
A glitch.

Enjoying
A tainted
Accomplishment.

As an audience
Of nymphs
Watch you
Create
For
The most glorious
Canvas.

This is
What
You do.

Ignore
The rest.

July 26th

A hard reset.

Blacked out.

A full immersion
Baptism
Before
Falling in
A pit
Of thorns.

Rescued
By friends.

Cared for.

Shown
The way
Back home.

After observing
The nature
Of things.

A beautiful
Peace.

A sublime
Surrender.

July 27th

Bruised.

Battered.

Beaten.

In a world
Of pain.

But
Never felt
Better.

A small price
To pay
For
A big
Upgrade.

A new
State of the art
Soul.

Equipped with
All
The bells
And whistles.

Ready
For battle.

Ready
To put in work.

Cleaning up
The dead
In the
Astral city.

Reaching
With an
Outstretched
Hand.

July 28th

Digging
And blasting
Through
The mountain
Of difference
That separates
Us.

Building
A tunnel
Of understanding.

Pushing
Through
The danger.

Not retreating.

Sensing
The light
On
The other side.

Just enough
Seeping through
The cracks.

To keep
Guiding us.

We will
Escape
To freedom.

July 29th

Sunup
To
Sundown.

A full day
Of labor
On the home
Front.

Working
The body.

Creating
Space
By discarding
The past.

The last
Promise kept
And word
To be
Honored.

You did
What
You said
You would.

Now
It's time
To move
Forward.

Transcending
And
Including this
Completed
Stage.

July 30th

Dragging
The decaying
Wishing well
Up
The hill.

Destined for
The dumpster.

Hoping
That
It has
Room for
One more
Wish.

Remember
That yours
Is the promise
I'm most proud
To have kept.

But
It's no longer
What sustains
Me.

We are
Free
Of each other's
Destinies.

Thank you.

All
Love.

July 31st

A cathartic
Release.

Emptying
Myself
Of that
Which
I don't
Need.

That
Which
Overfills
Me.

That
Which
Does not
Fulfill
Me.

A deliberate
Step
Backwards.

As I ready
To run
Forward.

Losing that
Which got stuck
Under
The boat.

As I leave
Shallow waters
For the deep
Sea ahead.

August 1st

A master
Of his craft.

An ageless
Romance forged
In timeless
Music.

A celebration
Of life
Love
And art.

It's what
Makes this
Such
A wonderful
World.

Where
Anything goes
When
Creativity reigns.

Hearts
Connecting with
Hearts.

True
Beauty.

August 2nd

A devastating loss.

A hero
To many.

A friend
To all.

Hard
As a rock.

Good
To the bone.

It's like
We're getting
Too used to
This.

When
Tragedy becomes
The norm.

And normalcy
Becomes
Unsteady.

When
Will it
Strike
Again?

What's
Lurking
Around
The corner?

Is anybody
Safe?

I don't know
Anymore.

August 3rd

A full day
Of fights.

Absorbing
Blows.

Stuffing
Take downs.

And emerging
Standing
With my hand
Raised.

Turning
The corner
As I
Make
My escape.

With
The red cardinal
Leading
The way.

Don't give me
The news

Of some world
That's not
Mine.

Tell me about
The truth
Of eternity.

August 4ᵗʰ

Just
A collection
Of appetites.

Hunger
Thirst
Lust.

Never
Can be
Sated.

An endless
Feeding frenzy.

Must
Overcome it.

Need
To outrun it.

Lord
You gave me
The insight.

Now
Give me
The strength.

I have achieved
Like
The scientist.

But
I need
To be fulfilled
Like
The artist.

August 5th

Between me
And my mind.

Lies
The root
Of the creative
Process.

The Holy Spirit
Working through
The murkiness
Of experience
Temperament
And personality.

Trying to
Maintain
A clear channel
And
Right
My wrongs.

While
The same wrongs
Wrote
The Psalms.

Needing
Brokenness
To appreciate
The fullness
Of God.

August 6th

Achieving
Goals.

Going
The distance.

A baker's dozen.

Without any
Half-stepping.

But
Still
Just a rung.

Near
The bottom
Of the ladder.

The ascender's journey
Is endless.

Literally.

So enjoy
The trip.

You
Will never be
Finished.

Until
You're finished
Being you.

August 7th

A toast
To the fallen.

Washed down
With memories
And regrets.

Chased by
The grisly details
Of reality.

Sometimes
Rain
Is just
Rain.

Other times
It's
The heavens
Crying.

Tears of joy
Over a
Brilliant soul
Continuing
His destiny
Of ascension.

Tears of sorrow
For all of us
Left
Forever
In his wake.

Cheers
John.

August 8th

Finished
Business.

Leaving
Room for
More truth.

Gifts
For the chosen.

For resisting
Temptation.

And yielding to
The adjuster.

Feeling
The pull
From the Father.

As the storm
Passes.

Dumping
Overboard.

What
You no longer
Need.

Move over
Little dog.

August 9th

A new light
Shines.

Where
Depletion stains
The eve
Of completion.

Actualization
After
The long stretch
Of hope.

Knowledge
Becomes
Crystalized.

With
A quantum leap
Of meaning.

And
An overflow
Of gratitude.

We truly
Ain't seen
Nothing
Yet.

August 10th

The power
Of the moon
Creeping
Out.

Feminine
Mystique
And the lure
It holds
Over you.

Like
A magnet
Drawing out
Virility
From
The metallic dust
Of manhood.

The origin
Of grace.

The strength
That comes
From beauty.

Be inspired
By
The confident
Energy.

But
Thou
Shall not
Covet.

August 11ᵗʰ

Departure.

Arrival.

Faces
And conversations.

Don't sweat
The small
Talk.

And
It's all
Small
Talk.

Unless
It's the Word
Of God.

And
Nobody wants
To talk
About that
Anymore.

Too stuck
In
Their universe.

Stop
Focusing on
Your breathing.

And
Focus
On He
Who gives
You
Breath.

When
A people watcher
Meets
A people feeler.

A nourishing
Exchange.

During
A long day
On the path.

With
A river
Too strong
To stop
Flowing.

And dragons
Reduced to
Just
A few
Gnats.

Self-love
Is
Easy.

When
You allow
Yourself
To be
Loved by
God.

August 13th

Spiritual
Gluttony.

A divine
Decadence.

Eat.

Pray.

Worship.

Meditate.

Again
And again
And again.

All
While bathing
In
The Word.

Surrounded by
The sublime
Setting
Of nature.

Emptying
The trash.

Filling
The well.

A mid-life
Overhaul.

As
I descend
The mountain
And travel
The valley
Of God.

August 14th

This is
Not
A reset.

It's
A fast
Forward.

Away from
The greys.

Back to
The blacks
And whites.

On
The wave.

With
The light
In front of
Me.

Darkness
Behind.

Ready to
Run.

The inevitable
Consequence of
Love is
Service.

I've picked
My side.

And
There's nowhere
Left
To hide.

August 15th

Made it
Out of
The labyrinth.

Of
New Age
Thought
And
Eastern
Mysticism.

Away from
Their orphaned
Prophets
And
Faulty
Assumptions.

Guided by
The hand
Of our
Holy Mother.

And
The heart
Of her
Son
Jesus.

It's only
One God
I sing to.

And three
Noble truths
I follow.

Be good.

Work hard.

Help others.

August 16th

A return.

The hardest
Part of
A trip
Is
Integrating all
You learned
In
Your everyday
Life.

But
Experience
Makes it
Easier.

The transcending.

The including.

The creating
Of
New patterns.

The building
Of
New shrines.

You're still
In
The afterglow.

Yet
To fully
Hit
The ground.

Prepare
For
Landing.

August 17ᵗʰ

A soldier
Of God.

Still able
To go
The distance.

Against
The future
He inspired.

While
A working class
Hero
Is still
Something
To be.

The stories
We tell
Ourselves
Can only
Be defended
For
So long
Until
The grand
Narrative
Overtakes
Us
All.

Ending
The chapter.

Closing
The book.

August 18th

You're playing
With fire.

When
You walk
The faith
That fractures
Families.

Baptism
By immolation.

Practicing
Tough love
Among the
Emotionally weak.

You've found
Your calm
Center
Amidst
A storm
Continuing
To rage.

A gentle breeze.

As
The lightning
Still
Crashes.

August 19th

You are
Here.

Where
Ideas become
Actualized.

In
The ease of
The process.

Gathering
The supplies.

After
The mission
Has been
Accepted.

Remove
All traces
Of the ego.

Stop
Being
A character
In
Your story.

Let go
Of
The narrative.

Embrace
The mindless
Mindfulness.

August 20th

Standing on
The shoulders
Of giants.

Seeing
Further.

But
Not liking
The view.

The post-coital
Comedown
Of creation.

When
You release
The spirit-gifted
Image
Into reality.

And are left
Naked
And
Empty.

Removed from
The equation.

Without
A trace.

Waiting for
What's next.

August 21st

Taught
A lesson.

For trying
To profane
A most
Sacred gift.

What
Was given
Can easily
Be taken
Away.

I am just
A tool.

Used
At His
Disposal.

For
His
Purposes.

Be
Weary of
Lust.

Before
It turns
The cake's icing
Sour.

Sweeten it
With your
Penance.

Hail Mary.

Our Father.

August 22nd

Without
Limits.

Running
Further
Distances.

Carrying
Heavier
Weights.

Pushing
The body.

Stretching it
From
The inside.

Enabling it
To house
A greater
Degree of
Spirit.

His will.

Soul.

Building
A cathedral.

In
A lonely
City
Without
A congregation.

As
The organ's pipes
Begin
To rust.

August 23rd

This
Is not
What brings
Me
Pleasure.

It's scratching
A limb
That was
Long ago
Amputated.

I made
A mistake.

Allowed
My truth
To get
Distorted.

Lost
In a prism
Of color.

Many
That
I'm blind
To see.

Stop
Relying on
The forgiveness
Of tomorrows.

Be merciful
With
Your todays.

August 24th

Replaying
Scenes from
A memory.

Until
I'm finally
Free.

Free
To give up
Control.

And
Accept
The joy
That comes with
Surrender.

The irony
Of exaltation
That only
Comes through
Humbleness.

The true
Earth
That only
The meek
Can claim.

The righteous
Trail
That only
A sinner
Could blaze.

August 25th

Palms
Bloody
And raw.

After taking
A tumble
In stride.

The magic
Begins
To wane.

Forcing
The faith
To stand
Alone.

One
Last stand
In
The city.

Before
Retreating to
The plain.

I've been
Roused by
The love
Supreme.

In its
Sublime
Chaotic
Glory.

But
Now
I seek
Only
The simple
The lucid
The Lord.

August 26th

A fitting
Feast for
The most high
Melchizedek.

Towing
The high line.

Stacking up
Blocks.

Visiting
The shrine
To hoarders
Of the past.

Watching
The art
That exists
Outside
The frame
And off
The canvas.

Hearing
The poetry
That can't be
Written down.

A slice of
A hidden
Empire.

August 27th

The mask
Has been
Peeled away.

Rebirth
And
Renewal.

Ready for
The lion's den.

The true
Face
Has been
Revealed.

But
The game
Is
No longer
Real.

As
The wound
Slowly
Heals.

Consolidation
And
Simplification.

Down on
Your knees.

Clues
To
The sorrowful
Mysteries.

August 28th

A sonic
Masterpiece.

Knocking down
All
The dominoes.

Joy
To
The world.

The Lord
Has
Come.

To
Teach us
That
An ideal school
Can't exist
In
An imperfect world.

But
An imperfect world
Can be
The ideal school.

To learn
And grow
And strive
To be
Perfect.

As
Our Father
In heaven
Is
Perfect.

August 29th

Check
The data.

But
Don't lose
The heart.

End
The summer
Well.

But
Be ready
For
The start of
Another adventure.

Enough
Talking.

I'm chomping
At
The bit.

Get me
In
The arena.

Let me
Fight
The bull.

I know
My meaning.

I know
My purpose.

Let me
Live it.

August 30th

A crisis
At the border.

As
The boat
Is stuck
In the harbor.

And you remain
A stranger
In all
Too familiar
Land.

A clown
That plays
It safe
Yields
The yawns
Of a bore.

The clown
That holds up
A mirror
Rips
To the very core.

But
A clown
That plays
It straight
Is
A path
That's surely
Yours.

August 31st

The sickness
Exposes itself
Fully.

But
No
Rash decisions
Were made.

I surrender
This
To you
God.

Provide me
The guidance
I seek
Tonight.

In
The morning
My thoughts
Will be
Your thoughts.

My words
Will be
Your words.

My actions
Will be
Your actions.

Have mercy
On
Me.

September 1st

I
Overcame it
All.

The hate
The anger
The sadness
The sin
The temptation.

I
Overcame it
All
Because
He
Lifted me
Up
And
Brought me
To
The other side
Of
It.

So
Here
I stand.

On
The other side
Of
It.

Healed
Whole
And humbled.

Personality found
Through
Ego-loss.

Exalted
Through
Surrender.

September 2nd

Another
Finish line
Crossed.

Before
Figuring out
What
Or who
You're racing
Against.

Time
No longer
Matters.

Nor does
Accomplishment.

So
Celebration
Seems
Pointless.

And
Rest
Becomes
Excessive.

You
Do it
Because
It's part of
Who
You are.

Who
He made
You
To be.

So
Do it
And
Be it
Fully.

September 3rd

Playing through
The pain.

As
The dirt
Gets in
Your stigmata.

The cross
Bouncing around
Your neck.

As
You keep
Hitting
Your mark.

The marathon
Has begun
And
Nobody
Was more
Prepared.

Enjoying
Each
Single step

After
Completing
The thousand mile
Journey.

September 4th

The legs
Get weary.

And
The mind
Falters.

The heart
Is not
As tough
As you
Thought
It was.

You're not
A fighter

You're not
A lover.

You're just
A guy
Living
Day to day.

Doing
The best
He can.

Knowing
You will
Always
Fall short.

Because
We all
Do.

Praying
For mercy
None of us
Deserve.

September 5th

The pieces
Are
In place.

Let
The game
Begin.

As
You get
More and more
Lost
In
The character
You
Created.

After
Escaping
The heart
Of darkness.

You're now
In
The belly
Of
The light.

With
No rescue
Coming.

No savior
In sight.

Apocalypse
Is
Now.

September 6th

Hell's bells
Are
Tolling.

As
The crusading knights
Fail
To take
The holy land.

History
May not
Repeat itself
But
It is
Certainly
Rhyming.

Cycles
Of progress
Spin
Upward.

While
Entropy
And chaos
Filter
Down.

It's all
Chutes
And ladders.

A game
Not worth
The risk.

September 7th

In
The clash
Of gladiators.

The righteous
And humble
Win
The day.

Putting
The art
Above
The accomplishment.

And
Class
Above
The conquest.

It is
Not personal.

It's
Business.

The business
Of mastering
Yourself
And proving
Who
You are.

Because
In the end
That's
All
There is.

September 8th

A jump
In levels.

Harder
To beat
The adversary.

He is now
Coming
At me
In forms
I'm not
Used to.

No longer
Hiding at
The far edge
Of my zone
Of proximal
Development.

He's out
In the open
Now.

Going
To require
A greater
Effort.

To stay
Ahead
Of him.

But
I'm trying
My best.

You see that
Right
God?

September 9th

And so
It begins.

The real
First day.

And
I more than
Made
The grade.

Now
It's just
A matter
Of maintaining
And sustaining.

Consistency.

Persistence.

Patience.

Three
Of
The things
I excel
At.

Three
Of
The things
I will
Need
Now
More than
Ever.

I
So
Got
This.

September 10th

Taking
Some punches.

Absorbing
Blows.

You
Now have
A better
Idea
What
You're up
Against.

Adjust.

Adapt.

But
Keep moving
Forward.

Stay light.

Unburden yourself
From
The weight
Of the past.

Stick
And move.

Stick
And move.

Avoid
The clinch.

Draw them
Into
Dark waters.

September 11ᵗʰ

The new
World order
Is
Officially
An adult.

The Illuminati
Is
As suburban
Now
As soccer
Moms.

And
Mini-vans.

While
The rebel
Is clean
Shaven
And kneels
At
A Sunday pew.

Radicalized
Amidst
The chaos
Of novelty
And flux.

Strange times
Indeed.

September 12th

It's surprising
How much of
Yourself
You get
Back
After
You surrender
It all
To Christ.

Parts
You thought
You had to
Give up
Now
Are
Exalted.

One of
The many
Joys
Of grace.

Jesus first.

Then
Others.

And lastly
You.

But
ALL
Of
You.

Nothing
Held back.

September 13th

Tonight
The fruits
Of hard work
And experience
Will be
Harvested.

As
The old man
Is not ready
To ride out
To pasture
Yet.

Not
When
He still has
Lessons
To teach.

And
Charges
Still willing
To listen.

Only those
Tethered to
The wisdom
Of
The past
Will not
Fly
Into
The furnace
Of
The sun.

September 14th

This is
No longer
A world
For
The cowboys
And acrobats.

We don't need
Showmen
And
Their circuses.

This is
A world
For
The blue-collar worker
Willing
To punch
The clock
And
Go
The distance.

All day.

Everyday.

Wearing
The adversary
Down.

Ready for
The judgement.

Raise
His hand
High.

September 15th

I would
Gladly
Give up
The fatted calf
For
My older brother.

But
Some people
Are lost
And
Never coming
Back.

Even
The holiest
Among us
Are slaves
To
Our appetites.

Filling
A gap
We know
Can only
Be filled
By God.

The gap
Between
Devotion
And
Complete surrender.

Between
Mere priests
And
Saints.

September 16th

The process
Begins.

The last ditch
Efforts
To prevent
Me
From getting
Here
Have been
Thwarted.

They were
Merely
Gnats
In the face
Of a
Charging stallion.

Broken
By God.

There is only
One master
To serve.

Serve Him
Shrewdly.

Serve Him
Righteously.

September 17th

Taking out
The trash.

The excess
That precedes
Success.

The waste
On
The path
Of
The chaste.

They see
The change.

They sense
The transformation.

But
Have
No clue
How far
This will
Go.

No longer
Fighting
It.

No longer
Fearing
It.

Embrace
The grace.

September 18ᵗʰ

An amber
Alert.

On
A red letter
Day.

Standing awkwardly
On
The purple
Fringes.

Having
Already stomached
More
Than you
Can handle.

All
They see
Is
The disciplined
Abstainer.

While
You feel
The pangs
Of
The shameful
Glutton.

Not
Your friends.

Not
Your family.

Just
Runners.

Pushing
Your pace.

September 19th

Losing
Footing.

Slipping.

Bracing for
A fall.

The weight's
Not
Too heavy.

But
You've been
Holding it
Up
For
Too long.

Afraid if
You put it
Down
You'll never
Pick it
Up
Again.

No one
Sees
The struggle.

No one
Is offering
A spot.

This one's
On you.

September 20th

Planting
Seeds of
A living
Faith.

Cultivating
A crop of
Mental
Toughness.

Harvesting
The joyful
Bounty of
Living for
The Lord.

By
His grace
Your soil
Was fertile.

And
He
Let love
Reign
Over you.

Removing
Your weeds
One
By
One.

Leaving
Fields
Of
Green
And
Gold.

September 21st

Pounding
The pavement.

Enjoying
The golden
Silence.

Listening to
The thoughts
Hidden in
The dark corners.

I'm not
Quite sure
What
I'm heading
Towards.

But
I'm going
Faster
In its direction
Everyday
Now.

Past
The point
Of
No return.

The vortex
Is sucking
Me
In.

September 22nd

Withdrawal.

Paying back
What
You borrowed.

A weary
Soldier
But not
A wounded
One.

Still marching
Forward.

Still carrying
The flag.

It's not
What your
Body
Feels like.

It's definitely
Not what
It
Looks like.

It's what
It
Can do.

Day
After
Day.

Further.

Heavier.

Faster.

September 23rd

Lazarus
Is everywhere.

Don't let
The guilt
Consume
You.

Or
Be
Self-righteous
In
Your deeds.

Start
Where
You are.

Forgiveness begins
With
The small.

Keep
Getting into
Shape.

And then
You will
Be taken
To
The mountain tops.

The majestic
Awaits.

September 24th

Lighter
And lighter.

Trimming away
All
The fat.

The process
Is
Absurd.

It only
Makes sense
Because
God is
Real.

The only way
To live.

Anything else
Would be
Even more
Absurd.

Still
Don't know
The destination.

But
I'm loving
The journey
More and more.

This is
My escape.

September 25th

Scraping away
At
The nether regions.

Removing
The waste
That resulted
From
The want.

The crane
Hoists
The load.

High above
The tree tops.

Out
With
The old.

In
With
The new.

Many paths
Could have
Been
Taken.

I took
The only one
Available.

September 26ᵗʰ

Back to
School.

It's all
Covered in
The syllabus.

Policy
And procedures.

Breadth
Of content.

A paper
Trail to
Nowhere.

In
A pointless
Game.

Any questions?

This is
The façade
You were
Looking for.

Makes you
Hopeful for
The future.

While
Underneath
Is still
Filth.

No
Hotter topic
Than
Worship of
False idols.

Bought
And sold
In
The marketplace.

With
The tokens
Earned
Through
Frivolous play.

With an ace
In hand.

To trump
All
The cards.

While
The shepherd
Leads
His flock.

Silently
From behind.

September 28th

Some
Easy nuts
To crack.

During
Some
Much needed
Rest
And relaxation.

After
An early morning
Rescue.

I'll be
Your pal
In the E.R.
Because
That's my
M.O.

Yet
Another glimpse
Behind
The veil.

Of all
The sickness
And pain.

That
Which
Makes
Us
Stronger.

September 29th

The world
Is not
Made of
Fire.

It's
Made of
Light.

I'm not
Mad as hell
I'm
Serenely
Accepting.

Everyone
Has their reasons
For entering
The arena.

The wise
Find theirs
For exiting.

It's
A fixed fight
For
Champs
And chumps.

With
Endless rounds
And
Crooked judges.

Might
As well
Tap.

September 30th

Can you
Hold
Or
Is this
An emergency?

The path
I've used
To walk
Away
Is well
Worn in
Both directions.

Maybe
This is
The time
There's
No
Going back.

An ending
In earnest.

I let go
Of more
Each time.

So there's
Less to
Come back to.

Travelling
Light.

October 1st

Tired
From
The day.

Exhausted
From
The season.

Functional disagreement
In close proximity
Is pain.

And
I keep
Making myself
More
Functionally
Disagreeable
To everyone
Around me.

Except you
God.

So
You better
Stay
Close.

You're
The only
Joy
I have.

You
Wanted it
That way
Right?

October 2ⁿᵈ

A distant
Tune.

A repetitive
Rhythm.

Not certain
Where
It is coming
From.

Or
If it's
Real.

What
Is this life
For?

Even
The willing
Servant
Yearns
To know
The purpose
Of
His servitude.

I know this
Is the end
Of something.

But
Of what?

The enigma
Of living
In
The moment
Is
Tiresome.

October 3rd

The feeling
Of forces
Focused
Against you
Is
An illusion.

It is
Just
Their insecurities
And yours
Hitting
Dead on.

You
Have been
And always will
Be protected.

Supported.

Guided.

Loved.

The last gasp
Of the desperate.

Let it be
Released.

For
It is
Finished.

October 4th

Picking up
The pieces
That
I helped
Knock down.

Of
A game
Spanning
Millennium.

Obnoxious.

Unsportsmanlike
Conduct.

Learn
The rules.

Don't let
Them in
Your head.

Display
Your mental
Jiu Jitsu.

A purple belt
Surrounded by
White.

But
Always
Bet on
Black.

October 5th

God
Speaks in
The book
Of Job.

But
Is he
Teaching
Or just
Bragging?

What
We need
Is
Consoling.

Everybody is
Sensitive.

We need
A divine
Hug.

To
Tell us
It's alright.

He was
With us all
Along.

We
Know it.

But
It's hard to
Feel it.

In this
Cold world.

That's
Getting
Colder.

October 6th

The animals
Receive
A blessing.

But
It's those
Holding
The leashes
That need
Redemption.

Mongrels
Guarding
The altar
From
Seekers
Of truth.

In
A children's game
The size of
The dog
Does matter.

Once shy
But
Never bitten.

Now
I'm shouting
From
The rooftops.

October 7th

Broken shards
Everywhere.

Buried
Amidst
The sands
Of the hourglass.

A sharp anger
Thrusts
Its way
To the surface.

But is
Quickly
Shown
Who's in charge
Now.

Control
Is needed
For
The daily lesson.

Chaos
Befits
The lessons
Of a lifetime.

The teacher
Has a home
In them both.

October 8th

Through
The eyes
Of a lion.

Eternity
Seems
So real
To me.

Death
Has been
Conquered.

The stakes
Of the old
Tent
Will be
Lifted
The moment
We are
At one.

Awaken
From
This dream.

Focus
On
The invisible.

Humble yourself.

Bathe in
The Jordan
Seven times.

Heal
The leper
Within.

October 9th

Beating
The devil
In the
Big battles.

But
Still
Losing
The small
Scraps.

Appetites
Will never
Be sated.

It's like
Chasing
After wind.

Don't live
For
The stomach
Or
Pleasures
Of the tongue.

This too
Is meaningless.

Find pleasure
In resistance.

The freedom
Of discipline.

October 10th

A call
For help.

As
The enemies
Seem to be
Breaching
The gates.

Looking around
But
No one
Appears
To be
On
Your side.

They're waiting
For you
To lose
It.

They're waiting
For you
To drop
The weight.

You'll prove
Them
Wrong
In spite of
Yourself.

I just
Wish
It didn't
Have to be
This way.

October 11th

It's overtime
And
You're
So over
Time.

Just
Give me
A moment.

The best defense
Is when
The other team
Has
No offense.

And
Being defensive
Is
So offensive.

No offense.

Nobody is
Going to
Win this.

But
Somebody is
Going to
Not
Lose it.

So
Hold on.

Time's
Almost
Up.

October 12th

I come
From away.

And
Land on
This rock.

To taste
All the flavors
That dull
The palette.

And hear
All the sounds
That deafen
The ears.

Among
The bright lights
And
Big city.

I see
Only
The small
And
Dimly lit.

Moths
Around
A lightbulb.

Knowing nothing
Of
The sun.

October 13th

Attraction
Is often
Just
Recognition.

I see you
Right now.

Not as
Someone
For my future.

But
A memory
From
My past.

Life.

World.

Dimension.

An individual
Or
A pattern.

That
I've experienced
Before.

How
Have you
Been?

You
Look like
You've translated
Well.

You
Do something
Different with
Your hair?

October 14th

An anniversary
Of heartache.

As
A flood
Of memories
Cause
The levies
To break.

The roller coaster
Is
Over.

But
Your legs
Are still
Quaking.

When
Soul mates
Become
Life lessons
Learned.

And
Old friends
Remain
Phantom itches
Scratched.

It's time
To bring
Your soldier
Home.

It's
Another man's
Fight.

October 15ᵗʰ

A wall
Of sound.

Reverberating.

Echoes
Of the past.

Heralding
The limits
Of human consciousness.

The edge
Of dialectics.

Thesis.

Antithesis.

Synthesis.

Again
And again
And again.

Until
It collapses
Into itself.

Creating
A wall
Of sound.

Reverberating.

Echoes
Of the eternal.

AUM.

October 16ᵗʰ

This is
Why
You came
Here.

This is
What
Got you
Stuck.

There is
No
Going back
Now.

The only way
Out
Is through.

Overindulge
Until
You seek it
No more.

Play out
Your fantasies
And see them
For what
They are.

Get sick
Off the
Sweetness
Of the
Samsara.

So
You can
Savor
The bitterness
Of the
Cross.

October 17th

The salt
Of the earth.

Adding
Seasoning
To the blandness
Of
Post-modernity.

A family Joad
Travelling
The wasteland.

Proudly
Showing
Their colors.

Waiting for
Any occasion
To rise up
To.

No obstacle
Is too
Great.

We'll still
Get them
Home.

Clearing
A path
For
The strong
And weak
Alike.

October 18th

The great
Pretender.

Silly
To a fault.

Interviewing
With sirens.

Immersed
In the glory
That is
Knowing humanity.

Your ship
Remains
Unharmed.

Sailing
To its goal.

Guided by
The cross.

Your faith
Is no
Deal breaker.

It's
The prize
Behind
Every door.

Waiting
To be
Opened.

October 19th

Stepping outside
The matrix.

To take
Three orbits
Around
Your world.

Seeing things
From
Afar.

Before
Plugging
Back in.

A dirty
Dozen.

Testing
The mind.

Quieting
Your thoughts.

The serene
Gentleness
That can
Only be
Achieved through
Disciplined
Mental toughness.

Invigorating
Exhaustion.

October 20th

An infant
Saint
Dressed in
White.

Joins
The congregation.

This is
Our faith.

Welcome.

Old fighters
Waving
The black
Flag.

Get
Knocked out
Of their
Prime.

This is
Our fate.

Beware.

In-between
Is life.

The shades
Of grey
Separating
Sin
From
Salvation.

This is
Our world.

Enjoy.

October 21st

Never forget
The rock
That
This church
Was built
Upon.

The rock
Of ages
And sages.

A mountain
Of hope
Rising
From these
Dark waters.

For all
The hopeless
Sinners
Trying
Desperately
Not
To drown.

Or
Be carried away
By
The current.

Just
Keep
Your toes
Up
And
Reach for
His
Outstretched
Hand.

October 22nd

It's
The blind
Leading
The blind.

As
The throne
Of the
One-eyed king
Is vacated.

No choice
But
To keep
Pushing.

Forward
Through
The dreariness
Of the
Season.

The foundation
Remains
Intact.

The structure
Is
Sound.

We will
Reach
Great heights.

Once
Time
Is right
Again
To build.

October 23rd

No longer
Know what
I'm running
From.

No longer
Care
Where I'm
Headed.

There's some
Strange
Voodoo
In the air.

And
I'm tired
From pulling
Out
All the pins.

I wrote this
Five times
Already
In my dreams.

Rough drafts
For
This reality.

Hoping
My waking
Life is
The best
Version.

October 24th

Was ready
To
Step out
Of
The ring.

Already had
The gloves
Off.

Recognized
The pattern.

And
Put them
Back on
In disgust.

I'm too strong
To let
Weakness win
This time.

The extra mile
Has become
Familiar road.

The future
Is
Overpowering
The past.

So
Stop thinking
About
Yesterday.

October 25th

An impasse
On the bridge.

A moral
Dilemma.

The world
Is
Group therapy.

Not everybody
Who makes it
Out
The maze
Follows
The correct
Path.

And
The destination
Is the same
For
The righteous
And
The rule-breakers.

With
Only pride
Separating
The two.

And
Pride is
The bigger
Sin.

October 26th

With
A little help
From
My friends.

Getting by.

Early
For
The water.

But
Late
For
The sky.

Making
The most
Out of
This land.

A tight
Squeeze
But
I made it
Out.

Down
The road
Of worship.

Taking
The exit
Of praise.

Hallelujah.

He did it
Again.

October 27th

A chance
Encounter
In
The rain.

Strangers
In
The market.

Made familiar
By
Their faith.

The temptations
Increase.

As
Your will
To resist
Grows
Stronger.

A flow
State
Of grace.

Develops
The soul
From within.

Walking
With
Weights on
In
The dark.

In order
To run
Freely
In
The light.

The state
Of
The union
Is
Only
Strong
Depending on
Who
Or what
You are
In union
With.

Those
In union
With
The self
Are slowly
Going mad.

Those
In union
With
The world
Are quickly
Losing hope.

Those
In union
With
Christ
Are marching
Together
In strength.

Oh how
I want
To be
In
That number.

October 29th

I
Ain't no
Joker.

Getting bored
Of what
Y'all
Throwing
At me.

You
Used to
Be my
Workout.

Now
You're just
My
Warm-up.

Keeping
The muscles
Fresh
For
The main
Event.

Waiting
For
The amateurs
To cool
Down
And
Get off
The mat.

Take
A bow
And
Make room
For
Your sensei.

October 30th

A farewell
To arms.

Raise
A glass
For
Another toast.

As
The next one
Moves
Along.

Leaving
The loyal
And
The lonely
In his wake.

Feeling
The visceral
Pain
And sting
Of
The needle
Entering
The skin.

Leaving
An indelible
Mark.

Of tigers
And children
Fighting.

October 31st

Seeing
The world
From behind
The mask.

A kaleidoscope
Of faces.

A dance
Of colors.

Humanity
Is so
Real
It's
Surreal.

Flirting with
The outer
Limits of
Sanity.

But
Knowing
The ledge.

A friendly
Face

Behind
Every demon
You
Confront.

Claws
And fangs
On all
The angels
Guiding you
Home.

November 1st

A day
For all
Saints.

From
The sanctified
To
The secular.

Fighting
For
The forgotten.

Standing up
To
The bullies.

An
Unstoppable
Hero.

Disarming
The bombs.

The world
Is still
Fallen
And
Broken
Beyond
Repair.

But
The faithful
Keep working.

Tending
The weeds
Until
The revelation
Is
Complete.

November 2nd

To all
The souls
I've loved
Before.

I don't need
A belt
To tell me
How bad
I am.

Just ask
Those
I bested
And
They will
Attest
To it.

Better yet
Ask those
Who bested
Me.

They'll tell
You
I went
Out
Swinging.

Shining
Bright
Like
A purple light
In
The darkness.

November 3rd

Ten
Hail Mary's.

Please Father
Forgive me.

I'm doing
The best
I can.

With
What
I have.

And
What
I think
I know.

I get
Dizzy
With
The wide
Pendulum swing
Between
Me
And
Living
For you.

Praying for
That stillness.

Where
Being me
Is living
For you.

The missing
Peace.

Found.

November 4th

The emptiness
That comes
From getting
What
You want.

A bitter
Taste.

Removed from
The rollcall
Of
The valiant
Knights.
Fighting
The good
Fight.

And
Lumped into
The purgatory
Of those
Seeking
Ease
And relief.

You
Are not
The person
You are
In
Your head.

Remember that
And
Stay humble.

November 5th

Back to
Standard.

Higher
Up.

Harder to
Maintain.

But
So very
Necessary.

Flipping through
The channels
Of reality.

Foraging through
Frequencies.

Equilibrium
Is hard
To tune
Into.

But
So very
Necessary.

Old hats
Don't fit
Anymore.

Safety nets
Loaded with
Holes.

Hard to
Escape
Familiar patterns.

But
So very
Necessary.

November 6th

Misguided
But
On
The right
Path.

Stuck
But
Building
Momentum.

A checkpoint
Is reached.

Lines
Are being
Drawn.

As
You
Stubbornly hold
Your pen.

Refusing
To take
A side.

Not hanging
On to
The old.

No complying
With
The new.

Drawing
A circle
In
The sand.

Defining
The boundaries
Of
Your loneliness.

November 7ᵗʰ

Sometimes
You have to
Let
Depression
Win
Some battles.

Just
As long as
You stay
Ahead of
The war.

The monster
Will
Never go
Away.

It is
Always
Lurking
In
The depths.

Waiting for
The right time
To surface
And strike.

The strongest
Warrior
Will eventually
Tire
And let
His guard
Down.

Roll with
The punches
And
Keep moving
Forward.

November 8th

On
The outskirts
Of productivity.

Disengaged
But focused.

Going through
The motions.

While moving
Gracefully
Through
This life.

Surfing
The samsara
Without
A shore
Worth
Landing on.

Waiting on
A delivery
The deliverer
Or
Deliverance.

Save me
From
This
Vanity.

November 9th

The eve of
The final
March.

The soldiers
Are
Armed
And
In place.

Childhood
Is lost
As family
Comes
Together.

Faith
Is solidified
As
Prayers are
Answered.

The preacher
Speaks
Of heaven
As
The widow
Still mourns.

The sky
Is clear.

The air
Is crisp.

The moon
Shines bright.

November 10ᵗʰ

When
Your words
Echo back
At you
You realize
Their emptiness.

Strong enough
To shoulder
The pain
Of
The long
Death march.

But
Only
To be
Led back
Where
You started.

Alone.

An overflowing
Cup.

Forged
In fire.

Earned experience.

But still
Alone.

Not
A friend
In sight.

November 11th

There is
Nothing more
Insidious
As when
The devil
Attacks you
Through
The words
Of
A loved one.

Taking advantage
Of
Their weakness.

To strike
Where
You are
Most vulnerable.

Reminds you
How real
This battle
Truly is.

And
How high
The stakes
Truly are.

And
How much
Work
Is left
To be
Done.

November 12th

It
Doesn't matter
That
Mercury
Is
In retrograde
As
It transits
Across
The sun.

Or
That
The full
Beaver moon
Looms large
In
The night
Sky.

The children
Are sick.

The adults
Are impotent.

It's a
Broken
Fallen
World.

Looking for
Answers.

That only
The faithful
Know.

November 13th

New maps
Are
Unlocked
For all
Too familiar
Territory.

It's
A different
Route.

But
You've been
Down
This road
Before.

Arriving
In time
For
The homily
To
Be read.

Everyday
Deserves
A happy
Ending.

And
It's
Always
Good
To hear
The good
News.

November 14th

My words
Have always
Come
From He
Who is
The Word.

My voice
From He
Who is
Speechless.

Just
Pick up
The pen.

Do
The work.

And
Get
Out of
The way.

A pure
Unprocessed
Creative
Process.

I'm not
The driver.

I'm not
The vehicle.

I'm just
A pilgrim
On
The road.

Going
Where
The ride
Takes me.

November 15th

Hitting
The wall.

After
Fitting in
The final
Piece of
The puzzle.

Crashing
But not
Burning.

It's all
Out there
Now.

There's nothing
You held
Back.

So
What's next?

Plowing forward
Or
Enjoying
A well-earned
Retreat?

Bulking up
Or
Slimming down?

Choosing
Your own
Adventure
Or
Floating in
The wind?

November 16th

Mother Seton
And
Saint Augustine
Pray for us.

Show me
A view of
Your
Shining city
On a hill.

For
I don't know
Who
I was
Back when.

When
The journey
Was more
Meaningful
And
The destinations
More
Distinct.

Before
The muddled
Meaninglessness
Of
Now.

And
Bittersweet
Sadness
Of
Later.

November 17th

An original
Sinner.

Listening for
The answers.

To
The unspoken
Questions.

Wearied by
The constant
Weight
Of discernment.

Just
Tell me
What
To do.

I will
Follow
Your orders.

But
I can't
See
What flag
I'm fighting
For
Amidst all
The fog
And haze.

So
Lord
Just
Sound
Your bugle
And
I will
Come
Charging.

November 18th

Welcomed
Home.

A wayward son
To
A dysfunctional
Family.

Confessing of
The wounds
I bore
During
My time
Away.

All of them
Self-inflicted.

A lifetime
Of guilt
Made into
A raindrop
Absorbed by
The ocean
Of
The Father's
Love.

What
A relief.

Now go
Enjoy life
And
Smile more.

November 19th

What's on
The other side
Of
The eye of
This needle?

You ask
Yourself.

As you
Confidently
Ride
Your camel
Through it.

A rambling man
Born rich
In spirit.

But short
On grace.

So enamored
With
The awesomeness
Of humanity.

You live
Alone
In solitude.

A hermit
Without
A habit.

Looking for
A new
Hobby.

November 20th

A dress rehearsal
For
The great
Charade.

A dog
And pony
Show.

When He
Was
Content with
Just
A donkey.

This path
Is mine
Alone.

So what
Are
All these
People
Doing here?

Still
Not comfortable
In my
Mystical
Body.

Got lost
In faith.

Resent
Being
Found.

November 21st

Calling for
Reinforcements.

In
A battle
That keeps
Slipping away
From me.

Asking for
Protection.

Because
The enemy
Won't
Stay away
From me.

Begging for
Forgiveness.

When
Heaven
Is so
Far away
From me.

Allow me
To feel
Loved.

Allow me
To feel
Accepted.

Allow me
To feel
Wanted.

Please show
A new way
To me.

November 22nd

Going faster
Where
I used
To go
Further.

Going further
Where
I used
To go
Faster.

The intersection
Of
Peak performance.

Steadily
Moving
Forward.

As
Others
Get tossed
To and fro
In the wind.

Fortifications formed
Through
Faithful prayer.

I must
Protect
This house.

November 23rd

God
Laughs at
Another one
Of
Your plans.

Can't even
Be mad
It's so
Common place.

There's
No rest
For
The wicked.

Running
So hard
Without
A Sabbath
In sight.

Your
Days off
Are becoming
Way
Too much
Work.

Time
To take
The foot
Off
The pedal.

Ease into
Cruise control.

Drive
Safely.

November 24th

I humbly ask
To
Be accepted
As
A candidate.

To seek
A further
Sharing in
The life
Of God's
Church.

But when
I search
My pockets
I have
Nothing
To offer.

Only
The shame
And embarrassment
Of
The life
I used
To live.

My salvation
Is
Not yet
Confirmed.

Though
Now
I walk
A straighter
Path.

November 25th

The dream police
Are
Asleep on
Their beat.

While
The surreal
Mindscapes
Disturb
Your rest.

Sleep is
The cousin
Of death.

But
You are
Far from
Being
In peace.

The territory
Is
Too new
For it
Not to be
Picked apart
And prodded.

Make sure
There are no
Hidden weeds
Before
The seeds
Are
Fully
Sown.

November 26th

Looking at
The skull
Of the buffalo
With
A mix of
Admiration
And awe.

It has
Drawn me
Away from
The futility of
Old patterns.

Allowing me
To march
Confidently
Forward.

Like bulls
On
Parade.

But
Always
Remaining
Humble.

Knowing
That I
Never would
Have chosen
This path
If
Not for
Grace.

November 27th

There's a lion
In your
Living room.

And
A cockroach
In the
Kitchen.

You found
Yourself
In the middle
Of
A wolf pack.

And returned
Without
A scratch.

Harmless
Like a dove
You left
Your bait
Behind.

Cunning
Like a serpent
You drew them
To
Your world.

A fisher
Of
Souls.

A reluctant
Grace.

An overwhelming
Gratitude.

For
An easy
Climb.

Through
A barren
Reality.

Of sensory
Input.

And
Soulless
Ritual.

Spared from
The trap.

But powerless
To warn
Others.

The agony
That comes
With acceptance.

The admission
Price
To
The kingdom.

November 29th

Towing
The fine line
Between
Depression
And
Transcendence.

Tired
Of your
Gas-lit anthem.

Just
Let me
Watch
The shadows
On
The cave walls
In peace.

I know
They're not
Real.

But
This is
What
I signed
Up for.

To drown
In
The illusions.

And
Resurface
Completely
Dry.

Jolted
Back to life
By God's
Defibrillator.

Colors
More vivid.

Sounds
More acute.

The eyes
Of strangers
Reveal
Multiple dimensions
And
Alternate universes.

A mandala
Of Mandela
Effects
Kaleidoscoping
Through
Eternity.

With one
Alpha
And one
Omega.

Jesus Christ
Our Lord.

December 1st

The advent
Of Advent.

Hitting
The ground
Running.

Taking care
Of
The unfinished
Business.

Getting
Ahead of
The storm.

When
Freedom
Has been
Long withheld
It is
Difficult
To
Properly enjoy
Freedom
Given.

It shouldn't
Take
So much
Effort
To force
Myself
To rest.

December 2nd

A day
That
Never happened.

Lost
In a world
Of sleep
And dreams.

A necessary
Sacrifice
To
The demon
Of
Depression.

Until
I am strong
Enough
To cast
Him
Out.

Along with
Everything
He
Feeds off
Of.

That
I'm still
Holding on
To.

The hardest part
On the road
Of recovery
Is when
You're reminded
Just
How much
Further
You still have
To go.

December 3rd

Back to
Square one.

But
Today's
Square one
Would
Have been
A distant
Mountain peak
Only yesterday.

Yet
That thought
Doesn't make
The fall
Any more
Palatable.

So
Forward
Climb.

Making sure
Your footing
Is
More secure.

Hoping
You have
The wisdom
To avoid
The same
Pitfalls
This time
Around.

December 4th

A soul
By any
Other name
Is still
A soul.

Eternal.

Beautiful.

Destined
To be
At
God's side.

For
We don't
Understand
This world
Any better
Than
They do.

We're all
Trying
To transcend it
In our
Own way.

Rejecting
The lies.

Refusing
The cake.

Snuffing out
All
The candles.

No wish.

December 5th

An equilibrium
Reached
Before
The next
Pull of
The pendulum.

Getting
A glimpse
Beyond
The stories
Of
The self.

Noticing
How high
The tides
Have gotten.

When
We all
Stopped
Paying attention.

Home
Before
The flood.

How grateful
I am.

To be
Home
Before
The flood.

December 6th

Hide
And
Go Seek
And
Charades.

We're all
Just kids
Playing games.

And telling
Each other
Stories.

Seeing shapes
And objects
In the clouds
Of vapor.

No one
Wants
To be
Reminded of
The ticking
Of
The clock.

Or
The line
In
The sand.

But
We can't
Sit on
Our thrones
Forever.

Tag.

You're it.

I already
Saw
What
I came
To see.

No need
To force
The issue.

I already
Covered
A lot
Of ground.

No need
To extend
The trip.

There
Will always
Be
Unfinished business.

Enjoy
The rest
When
It comes.

There
Will always
Be
Empty words.

Embrace
Meaning
Where
You find it.

Keep
Compounding
Interest.

December 8th

A cold wind
Blowing
Over
A partially
Frozen
Lake.

Knocks you
Out
Before
Your time.

Just after
Hope
Finally
Arrives.

And
You
Get on
Your knees
And
Pray for
Completion.

Fearing
That
You're not
Actually
Incomplete
But
Broken.

Beyond
Repair.

But
Still being
Put to
Good use.

December 9th

A nonstarter
With
Too many
Cooks
Under
The hood.

Hopes
Dashed
Again.

As
The cries
Of the earth
Become
An all
Too familiar
Sound.

Does pain
Have to
Be
The only
Path
To surrender?

Do only
Those who
Suffer
Seek
Forgiveness?

Why does
The prophet
Only speak
Of joy
After
Destruction
And
Damnation?

December 10th

They.

They
Don't know
The pain
They're causing.

They
Don't know
What's
At stake.

They
Are not
The future.

They
Are symptoms of
A broken
Now.

They
Are sadness.

But
They
Are beautiful.

They
Are still
God's children.

They
Can be
Saved.

They
Can be
Forgiven.

They
Can be
Redeemed.

They.

December 11th

Out on
The fringes
While
Getting to
The heart of
It all.

I had
A lot of
Fun
Avoiding
My destiny.

But
Didn't know
Joy
Until
I fully
Embraced it.

Just because
You're
An open
Book
Doesn't mean
Everybody
Wants to
Read it.

Keep shining
Your light
In
The dark.

The Miller
Will tell
His tale
In
The end.

December 12th

Always
Take
The stairs.

They are
Your
Quickest way
Down
And out.

Always
Look for
The stars.

They will
Point
The way
Up
And in.

What
A world
We're living
In.

When
The common
Sense peddlers
Have
The rarest
Jewels.

Attracting
Travelers
From
A far.

Who forgot
Joy
And
Laughter.

December 13ᵗʰ

Your past
Comes back
To arrest
You.

But
None of
Your demons
Are around
To press
Any charges.

So
You're
Getting off
Due to
Good behavior
And time
Already served.

Your future
Peeks in
During
The arraignment.

Looking
Sexy
As
Ever.

Buckle up.

It's going
To be
A glorious
Ride.

December 14ᵗʰ

You're on
The path
But
You're not
There
Yet.

Following
The revealed
Route.

Knowing
There is
No going
Back from
Here.

As
The trail
Gets
Narrower
And narrower.

It becomes
Easier
For
Others
To pull
You
Into
The brush.

Just keep
Looking to
The cross.

Don't blow
Your shot.

And
Blaze
On.

348

December 15th

Trying
To wrap
It all
Up.

But
There will
Always be
Loose ends.

Forcing festiveness
Unto
A commerce-driven
Chore.

Why
Do I
Always
Find myself
Here?

Is improving
In the way
I repeat
The same
Patterns
Really
Improvement?

Make me
Strong enough
To
Get off
The cycle.

December 16th

Memories
Of kissing
A fool.

As
Everybody is
Talking about
The good
Old
Days.

But
Things
Never really
Were
The way
They were.

A Mandela
Effect
Of emotions.

Focusing on
The joys
And
The sorrow
While
Forgetting
The boredom
And
Drudgery.

A highlight reel
Of
Delusions.

December 17th

A sheet
Of ice
Covers
The world
As things
Really
Begin to
Heat up.

But
I remain
Cool
And
Mild.

Chasing
My dinner
With
Psalms
And
Proverbs.

A chicken-salad
Sandwich
With
Jeremiah.

Thessalonians
Too.

A hungry
Infant
Sucking up
The nourishing
Truth.

In
No hurry
To be
Weaned off
God's
Word.

December 18th

No matter
How long
It's been.

And
How far
From
Your thoughts.

The anger
Still
Remains.

Residue
From
The ultimate
Betrayal.

A reminder
Of what
You could have
Succumb to.

But
You resisted.

As hard
As
It was
You resisted.

Choosing
Love.

Choosing
Faith.

Choosing
To forgive
The forces
That robbed you
Of
Your world.

Happy anniversary.

December 19th

In
A world
With
An increasing
Amount
Of
Gray areas.

It's becoming
More and more
Important
To pick
A definitive
Side.

Chaos
And order
Can't
Coexist
Unless
There's
A strong
Line
Separating
Them.

And
We will
Each
Have to
Decide
Which
Is which.

Accepting that
Your order
May be
Chaos
To another.

December 20th

Can't say
I sprinted
Through the
Finish line.

But
I wasn't
Limping
Either.

The brisk
Steady
Pace
Of someone
Used to
Going long
Distances.

Still feeling
The need
To fit
In.

But
Wanting
So much
More
To be
Free
Of
It all.

This
Is not
Who
I am
Anymore.

Can
Anyone else
See
That?

December 21st

Didn't
Heed
The warning.

Was
Fooled by
A false
Finish line.

Had
To be
Reminded
Just
How far
We have to
Go.

The shortest
Day.

But
The night
Is still
Long.

And dark.

With
The light
Of
The holy fathers
Refreshing
The weary
Souls.

Wisdom
From
The watchmen
Of
A future
Past.

December 22nd

It will
Take
More than
A smoke-filled
Sky
To obscure
The beauty of
This day
In
The neighborhood.

Blossoming with
Cheerful
Anticipation.

Before
The anticipation
Turns to
Anxiety.

The anxiety
To
Reality.

Reality
To
Disappointment.

Disappointment
To
Emptiness.

The roof
The roof
Is
On fire.

We
Don't need
No
Water.

December 23rd

Everybody
Talks about
The light
At the end
Of
The tunnel.

But
No one
Tells you
About
The darkness
At the beginning.

The doubt
About
Where
You're heading
Into.

The regret
Over
What
You're leaving
Behind.

The fear
Of knowing
It's
The only
Way.

Let me
Tell you
About
The darkness
At the beginning
Of the tunnel.

It's all
Worth it.

In
The end.

December 24ᵗʰ

After
The greatest
Story
Ever told
Everything else
Can only
Strive for
Runner up.

A retelling
Or
A remix.

A rehash
Or
Rust
Falling off
The only
Truth
There is.

Imitation
Is not
Art.

Inspiration
Is.

Artists
Need not
Aspirations.

Only
Worship.

So let's
Get down
On
Our knees.

December 25th

He came
To us
In
Human form
To show us
The divine
Face
Of mercy.

In
The lowliest
Places.

Where
Even water
Does not
Reach.

Grace
Will find
You.

Bringing you
To
Your knees.

First
In surrender.

Then
In submission.

Finally
In joy.

With beams
Of love
Radiating from
Your chest.

Shouting
Jesus
I trust
In you.

December 26ᵗʰ

The dog days
Are
Over.

Run to
Your family.

Run from
Your family.

Run for
Your family.

Just
Keep running.

A season
Of wrapping things
Up
Is yielding to
A season
Of opening
New boxes.

New expectations
And
Potentialities
That
Can never
Be returned
Or refunded.

Light
A candle
And
Pray for
A future
That
Can't be
Prevented.

December 27th

The road
Is long.

But he
Is not
As heavy
As I
Anticipated.

Your survived
But
Your edges
Have grown
Softer.

Weary
But not
Sick.

Renewed
But not
Refreshed.

In need of
Rest.

In need of
Comfort.

In need of
Distance.

Taking
The backward
Steps
Needed
To prepare
To leap
Forward.

December 28th

I must
Look funny
To all
The caterpillars
Struggling
To get
Their way
To the top.

As
I spin
My cocoon
In solitude.

Having to
Give up
More
And more
As
My labors
Intensify.

The artificial
Light
From
Their world
Growing
Dimmer
And dimmer.

And
Only when
I embrace
Complete darkness
Will I
Be blinded
By
The brilliance
Of
The Son.

December 29th

West
Of Williamsburg.

Just east
Of Eden.

Listening to
The gospel
Of John
And
The ageless
Wailings
Of Pharaoh.

Called
To walk
The chosen
Path
Which is
As new
To me
As
It is
Old fashioned.

Carrying
The cross
Through
The crowds
Of humanity.

Transcending
The world.

But not
Giving up
My worldliness.

December 30th

People
Walking around
With
Worried looks.

Finally
Realizing
That
This is
The time
Before
The deluge.

While
In
My city
The water
Is already
Up to
My knees.

As I
Playfully
Splash about
Like
The dolphins
Following
The ark.

Leaving it
To
The Noah's
To save
The world.

December 31ˢᵗ

It's midnight
Somewhere.

The moment
Is now
Everywhere.

The end
Of something.

The beginning
Of something
Else.

What else
Is
New?

Twenty years
Ago
You were
Somewhere.

Twenty years
From now
You'll be
Somewhere
Else.

Right now
You are
Right here.

Happy
New
Year!

Printed in the United States
By Bookmasters